T0341215

The Business Developer's Playbook

Relationship Selling Principles and
the DNA of Dialogue Selling

This book is an absolute must-read. It's not a book about "selling" in the limited way we generally think of that word, it's about influencing outcomes and making a difference, both to your life and success, and to the lives of others. Buy it, read it, and dip into it again, and again, as you encounter different circumstances. It's an Aladdin's cave of treasures. I wish I'd read it 40 years ago.

Professor Robin Stuart-Kotze
Chairman, Behavioural Science Systems Ltd.

As a health practitioner, I use my hands to dialogue with the body to support health, negotiating with restriction patterns in muscles and tissues, inviting space, opening to better circulation in the system. As a dancer, I dialogue with the music and with the audience, negotiating different movements as the music rises and falls, and as the audience attention comes closer or settles deeper; including the presence of all these elements is what helps me create my dance.

Communication, dialogue, negotiating is happening all the time in all facets of life and language is diverse. Peter Nixon's book reveals the fine art of communication and negotiation, reaching out beyond the boundaries of individual ideas to create relationships in every field of life; a practical guide to living and working harmoniously, peacefully. Everything we do in life can be a graceful dance, and this book teaches us about meeting without conflict. Peter is giving us what we really need, especially all the world's leaders and politicians.

Zia Nath
Founder, Quanta Health Care Solutions and Realms of Dance

When I set up my consultancy I had a so many questions about business development that I did not know where to turn. Peter's book has helped answer all my questions. If you want to feel like you are in a casual conversation with an internationally experienced consultant who is fast-forwarding your learning with his twenty plus years' experience, then you need to read *The Business Developer's Playbook* now.

Stuart Gerrard
Managing Director, Innovate to Operate

The Business Developer's Playbook

Relationship Selling Principles and the DNA of Dialogue Selling

By
Peter Nixon FCPA-CA

A PRODUCTIVITY PRESS BOOK

First edition published in 2019
by Routledge/Productivity Press
711 Third Avenue New York, NY 10017, USA
2 Park Square, Milton Park, Abingdon, Oxon OX14 4RN, UK

Printed on acid-free paper

International Standard Book Number-13: 978-1-138-32258-5 (Hardback)

Library of Congress Cataloging-in-Publication Data

Names: Nixon, Peter, 1961- author.
Title: The business developer's playbook : relationship selling
principles and the dna of dialogue selling / Peter Nixon.
Description: New York : Taylor & Francis, [2019] |
Includes bibliographical references and index.
Identifiers: LCCN 2018020496 (print) | LCCN 2018027216 (ebook) |
ISBN 9780429446542 (e-Book) | ISBN 9781138322585 (hardback : alk. paper)
Subjects: LCSH: Selling. | Business communication. | Negotiation.
Classification: LCC HF5438.25 (ebook) | LCC HF5438.25 .N59 2019 (print) |
DDC 658.85--dc23
LC record available at https://lccn.loc.gov/2018020496

Visit the Taylor & Francis website at
http://www.taylorandfrancis.com

This book is dedicated to all of you who helped me learn the essential skills, behaviours, and methods outlined in this book. You know who you are and some of you are specifically mentioned herein.

I also dedicate this book to professionals everywhere who will toil and study to master their profession only to learn that one of the most important skills needed to succeed, the ability to sell ideas and services to others, was likely absent from their training and will need to be learnt on the job. Hopefully this book will speed your learning, minimise mistakes, and maximise success.

If nothing else, remember, the solution is in the dialogue.

Contents

Preface

This book is testament to persistence and an unbending belief if you want something strongly enough you'll find a way to get it. When I started my negotiation and leadership consultancy in Hong Kong in the early 1990s, market surveys told me there was a need for what I was offering but I had three problems: the market didn't know me, I didn't know the buyers in the market, and most challenging of all, I didn't know how to sell.

Following ten very enjoyable years auditing multinational corporations (MNCs) in Canada, Switzerland, and Greater China, I declined partnership at Coopers & Lybrand (C&L is now the C in the world's largest auditing firm called PwC) and I took up the challenge of opening the Asian office for Behavioural Science Systems, the world-class UK leadership development firm which C&L hired at the time to help strengthen the leadership of their partners and managers around the world. In Hong Kong, where I landed in 1989, leadership and negotiation were the two most important "soft skills" in need of development. The firm in China then numbered 400 professionals and today is well over 10,000.

So, with the optimism and vigour typical of all new entrepreneurs I toasted the launch of Behavioural Science Systems Asia (BSSA) then watched as my UK-based partners flew back to their established homes and clients in the UK. Dr. Robin Stuart-Kotze, founder of Behavioural Science Systems and world-renowned leadership expert, was the first to depart. With his engaging smile, Robin said everything would work out fine and invited me to call him if I had any questions. My other partner, Dr. David West, who had been head of sales for Rank Xerox Europe and, like Robin, was a distinguished author in his own right, departed a day later. Before David departed Hong Kong, we met at Cinta-J restaurant in Wan Chai for a memorable last conversation: "David, I became an accountant because I didn't want to sell but now I have to sell and I'm okay with that but what should I do?" David wrote something down on a napkin about suspects and prospects and then he was off. Much of this book is what I learnt after my brief introduction to suspects and prospects.

After David and Robin left Hong Kong, I sat in my home office wondering how I was going to pay the bills for my rapidly growing family. My wife and I had just adopted our first child and we were in the process of adopting our second when we learnt my wife was pregnant with our third child. Going from a solid career in a big firm and a regular pay cheque to no pay, no clients, and rapidly rising family expenses caused two reactions. At first, I would find myself waking in the middle of the night in a sweat wondering how I would succeed. Then, realising worry and fatigue weren't going to help, I set about learning what I needed to do to win business and sell the services I knew the market needed. This book contains the best practices and principles I learnt after realising sales need dialogue, negotiation, and action (DNA) not worry and fatigue.

As one of the early leadership and negotiation entrants into Deng Xiao Ping's booming pre-handover Hong Kong, I had a lot of work ahead of me. Find buyers, understand their needs and wants, make proposals, introduce my world-class partners, and learn how to become an expert in my own right, all at the same time. Originally, my plan was to launch my business as a service line of C&L but when the C&L partners got cold feet, I was so far down the road launching the business that I just jumped in. I was so convinced I would succeed I named my company Potential Limited. In the early days of my new business, I met lots of suspects, some of whom were prospects and some of whom became clients. I didn't really know what I was doing but it seemed to be working.

"YOU WON'T SUCCEED"

Anyone who has run their own business will recognise that my sunny optimism had yet to encounter the inevitable downturn of the business cycle. The more I pushed into the market the more I began to meet naysayers who thought I wouldn't succeed and that I should return to working for my old firm. Overly risk-averse people see problems in high resolution yet downgrade opportunities staring them in the face.

One such naysayer and prospective client was KPMG, another of the "Big Four" accounting firms (the others are PwC, EY, and Deloitte). I thank the partners at KPMG Hong Kong for telling me several years after launching my business, "We thought you'd fail when you launched your consultancy but now you have a blue-chip client list around the world so you must be doing something right. Our partners and managers need to learn how a 'one-man band' can outperform an international firm". It was in response to their request that I designed and ran my first business development training. Soon the word spread and I was flying around the world providing business development training for professionals of all descriptions. This book explains all those things I wish I knew when I started my business and asked, "what should I do to sell?"

WHO SELLS PROFESSIONAL SERVICES?

Figure 0.1 shows professional service providers needing to sell.

WHY NOW?

Several people ask why I wrote about negotiation, dialogue, and culture before writing this book on business development even though market demand suggests this book has the greatest potential to outsell the other titles? It was luck and timing that matched me with my publisher John Wiley & Sons in 2003 when I approached them to share my negotiation experience with the world because Wiley were looking for a book on

Engineers
Architects
Tax Specialists
Lawyers
Private Bankers
Auditors **Dialogic**
Consultants **Sales Process:**
Artists **How to create,**
Trustees **manage and**
Accountants **maintain**
Advisors **productive**
Solicitors **relationships**
Corporate & Investment Bankers
Asset & Facility Managers
Designers
Property & Insurance Agents
Medical Professionals
Brokers

FIGURE 0.1
Professional service providers.

negotiation to complement their new series on mastering business in Asia. After that successful beginning Wiley then contracted me to write two more books: *Dialogue Gap* (2012) and this title, *The Business Developer's Playbook*. Recognising lack of dialogue as the leading issue of our time, I wrote and published *Dialogue Gap* next. This book earned significant acclaim and further fuelled my international speaking, training, and consulting assignments. Dialogue and negotiation are integral to successful business development and I encourage you to read these two books. The book you are holding in your hands touches upon dialogue and negotiation but focuses mainly on the action part of the DNA (what to do) and, when taken together, the three books respond to the question I posed years ago when I started this business, "what should I do to sell myself, my ideas, and my professional services?"

SELLING IS NOT MARKETING

My formative years working in the Big Four accounting firms taught me that accountants don't know much about selling, nor should they since accountants and sales professionals come from completely different professions with different core competencies. However, when professionals try to sell their ideas to "prospects" they need to know how to sell. This book is written in part with my fellow accountants in mind. They sigh with relief when I start my workshops by saying, "I became an accountant because I didn't want to sell".

Many professionals' concept of selling or business development is actually marketing. This is because selling was a dirty word and began with printing brochures and leaving them at reception where clients could take them away and read them. As firms developed they hired business development people to create mailing lists and push their brochures to client by post. Now these same brochures are fancy digital productions emailed to clients or shared via social media but the accountants sending them still conceive this to be selling when in fact it is marketing. Although it is valuable to market your professional services by leveraging the internet and other channels, this does not replace the need for selling. Taking actions to create, strengthen, and maintain relationships while surfacing and responding to the needs and wants of your clients is how you sell yourself, your ideas, and your services. Marketing can open doors and bring you fame but selling is what pays your bills. In this book, you will learn my business development tips and Relationship Sales Principles outlining the actions you need to take to sell. None of my tips and principles tell you to publish and distribute brochures outlining your services because this book is about sales not marketing.

DIGITAL SELLING

Digital communication, including getting leads, getting known, online dialogues, etc., are all commonplace in the public and private sectors today. Despite this there is nothing better than face-to-face dialogue to build trust and understand respective needs and wants. Skype, Messenger, WhatsApp, Facetime, and other apps allow for face-to-face dialogue and new sales channels are being created all the time for you to sell and market your services. Despite all these new tools we still need the right actions. My partners from Behavioural Science Systems will remind you that ultimate success requires getting the behaviour right. This book outlines in simple terms the behaviours still needed in our era of digital communication. It is important to remember that sales need trust and trust begins with dialogue. The bigger the deal the more important the dialogue. It takes time, in person, to build the relationships upon which you will build your business. This time cannot be replaced by tweets or posts but I also touch upon the important role digital communication plays in enhancing our business development efforts today.

CULTURE

Since publishing *Dialogue Gap* in 2012, the publishing industry has been through very turbulent years. Bookshops have closed just about everywhere and readers are reading fewer books than before. The good news is that after several years of decline, book sales are on the way up again and publishers are seeking authors. During this turbulence my publisher, John Wiley & Sons, waived their right to my third book and I was free to write whatever I wanted and publish with whomever was interested. I took advantage of work in New Zealand to write my third book entitled *Corporate Culture: Hurdles to Being #1 in the Private and Public Sectors Today* (Potential Limited, 2018), outlining, in my experience, the difference between winning organisations and their followers. Getting the organisational culture right is important for every successful sales organisation and this book addresses these questions too. It isn't all about money and making the sale and once this is clear to you and your staff, clients remember you and return to work with you much more than your competitors.

I hope you find my stories and lessons learnt valuable for selling yourself, your ideas, and your services around the world. Like other business development professionals, I am always learning and I value your questions and the chance to work with you and your organisation to help you realise your potential while helping others realise theirs.

Acknowledgements

I acknowledge people throughout the text for teaching me what I have learnt about business development but for those of you who helped me produce the final product, I extend a special thank you. It is a truly international effort and I believe the resulting work will be appreciated by business developers around the world.

Once I accepted to share what I had learnt on this topic in the form of a book, I jumped in wholeheartedly. The resulting draft outline was the first time my publishers stepped in to correct my vision for this book. I thank CJ Hwu, whose early feedback led to the realisation I really had two books planned, one on business development and one on corporate culture (the corporate culture book is still in development).

With my outline refined, CJ kindly referred me to her colleagues in New York and London but they, along with three other leading publishing houses told me business development didn't fit their current focus. As I remind you in this book, good business developers never give up, and despite hitting five dead ends, the resulting delay gave me the time to discover Routledge who was referred by Hetty Einzig, another Routledge author and fellow consultant in the UK. Hetty's referral led me through two other people and eventually to Lam Yong Ling, a Singaporean whose approach to bringing old world texts to twenty-first century readers, was the most refreshing change I'd seen in publishing since the advent of digital readers.

I had finally met a publisher who accepted the reality that few executives today have the time or interest to read books the way they used to. Lam Yong Ling introduced me to her colleagues Barry Clarke and Chia Jie Sin ("JS") in Singapore and to Naveen Rao in Mumbai, all of whom expressed excitement to work with an author wanting to embrace the digital world and produce enticing "digital snacks" appropriate to the twenty-first century reader.

The race to digital however needed a book and for this I thank Michael Sinocchi in New York City for recognising the international potential of this book. Yet again publishers saw what was needed and Michael recognised the need for a "playbook" type reference manual for business developers on the go so this is what we produced. The hard work of editing fell to Lisa Keating at Deanta and Robert Sims, Katherine Kadian, and the rest of the team at Routledge for making me look like a real writer. To all of you, I have to thank you. Now onto the digital snacks. ☺

Author

Peter Nixon provides training, advice, and inspiration for current and emerging leaders to achieve optimal outcomes through dialogue. As creator of The Potential Dialogue System, he has helped thousands of private and public sector leaders achieve optimal outcomes in over 500 organisations and 60 countries. Peter's slogan is "The solution is in the dialogue" and his philosophy is that "we have a duty to realise our potential while helping others realise theirs" (Potentialism).

He is founder and managing director of Potential Limited and author of several books including: *Dialogue Gap: Why communication isn't enough and what we can do about it fast* (John Wiley & Sons, Singapore, 2012) (SCMP: "One of the best business titles published this century"), *Negotiation: Mastering Business in Asia* (John Wiley & Sons, Singapore, 2005), *The Business Developer's Playbook: Relationship Selling Principles and the DNA of Dialogue Selling* (Taylor & Francis, USA, 2018), *Corporate Culture: Hurdles to being #1 in the private and public sectors today* (Potential Limited, Hong Kong, 2018), and *The Star Negotiator Casebook* (Potential Limited, Hong Kong, 2008). Peter is also creator of the popular Dialogue Playing Cards, which featured in Cathay Pacific's in-flight duty-free magazine.

Peter has worked with thousands of leaders advising on sales, sourcing, strategy, change management, family business, relationships, talent management, public sector, bilateral negotiations (Iran–US, Israel–Palestine, Malaysia–Thailand, Aceh–Java, Tibet–China, Sunni–Shia, Hong Kong–China), hostage negotiations, religious conflicts, regulatory change, compliance, shareholder disputes, mediations, and more. Peter's early career was spent auditing for PwC (C&L) in Montreal, Geneva, and Hong Kong.

Peter's workshops are popular for their pace, practicality, humour, and engagement and are often rated the best workshops people have ever attended. He advises mainly inside organisations but also teaches public courses at management institutes, chambers of commerce, universities, schools, and colleges around the world. Peter is CUHK (MBA) professor of Business Negotiation and visiting professor at HKPolyU, McGill, SFU, and Bishop's. He is also course director of HKICPA's Financial

Controllers' Programme; has appeared on TEDx, CNBC, Discovery Channel, TV5, TVB, and Media Corp. and has been showcase speaker globally for YPO and EO. His clients have received awards for his work including Colgate President's Award, HKMA Training Award nominee, and recently Potential was named Best Independent Change Management Consultant 2018 in the Hong Kong Business Awards hosted by APAC Insider Magazine.

Peter has been detained in Bahrain, locked up in Tehran, deported from Austria and India, hit by lightning in a small plane in the Arctic, survived roadside shootings in Aceh, bombings in Pakistan, 7/7 in London, slept with lions in Africa, survived bear intrusions and forest fires in Alberta, nearly broke his neck playing ice hockey, and led his small business through the ravages of the Asian Currency Crisis, Bird Flu, SARS, and the Great Recession. He joined a million Indian worshippers at Pushkar's Mela (Camel Fair) where pilgrims achieve eternal salvation if they step in the lake during November's full moon, which he did, but despite this, he still gets sick and pays taxes.

Peter was born and raised in Montreal, married in Geneva, and moved to Hong Kong in 1989 where he and his wife Marie raised their three children. Peter enjoys music ("the best form of dialogue"), reading (sociology, economics, religion), travel (to reach 100 countries), outdoor adventure (to connect with nature) and time with family and friends. Peter is immediate past chairman of Discovery Bay International School, Dean's advisor at McGill's Faculty of Education and to the School of Religious Studies. He is also director of McGill's Martlet Foundation in HK, Trustee of Outward Bound Hong Kong, Hong Kong Head of the Asian Cabinet of Bishop's University, and a member of the governance committee of UNICEF Hong Kong. He is a Fellow of the Hong Kong Institute of CPAs and has degrees from Bishop's (BBA), McGill (GDPA), and Leicester (MSc). He has also studied at Alberta, Harvard, INSEAD, and Fielding. He is a Canadian Chief Scout (1st TMR) and Knight of Tamara.

1

What Are You Selling?

Before diving into the DNA of selling, it is valuable to step back and ask yourself "what are you selling?" Most non-salespeople conceive of selling in terms of what they have experienced when confronted by salespeople trying to sell them products such as life insurance, savings plans, and consumer goods. The aggressiveness of product salespeople who put their need to sell ahead of the buyer's need to buy leaves a bad taste in the mouth of most buyers. When you look a little deeper you realise these salespeople push products which pay them the greatest commission and are themselves pushed by sales directors to meet monthly sales targets and earn handsome bonuses if the targets are achieved. When pushed by my life insurance agent to buy yet another life insurance policy I asked him "how many lives do you think I have?"

This book is not about selling products, it is about selling yourself, your ideas, and your services. If the English language were more refined it would have different words for selling inanimate products versus living things (like people, ideas, services) because the two are very different. You need only think about buying dog food versus buying a dog. The dog food remains the same over time, whereas the experience of owning a dog varies considerably from puppy to mature dog.

Despite the significant differences between selling inanimate and living things, we tend to call both selling, although sometimes people refer to the latter as influencing, negotiation, or even conflict resolution. And although both types of selling appear similar, selling products differs from selling yourself, your ideas, or your services in two important ways:

1. Product buyers normally understand what they are buying either physically (e.g. consumer products) or contractually (e.g. financial products) before investing and their ownership experience varies little if at all during the life of the product.

2. People who buy you, your ideas, or your services can only imagine what life would be like if they follow you, and because you, they, and the situation change over time, their "ownership experience" varies considerably over time.

Buyer experience: Inanimate products versus living ideas and services

	Buyer Experience Before Acquisition	Buyer Experience During Life of Acquisition
Inanimate acquisitions = products	Can see, hold, test-drive, understand contractually	Mostly consistent
Living acquisitions = Self, ideas, services	Mostly imagined	Can vary significantly

Examples comparing inanimate versus living acquisitions:

- Buying dog food versus buying a dog.
- Buying dog medicine versus buying veterinary services.
- Buying accounting software versus hiring an accountant.
- Buying new office furniture versus buying the ideas of an interior designer.

The following living situations are all considerably different from each other but everyone encounters some of these situations during their lifetime, either as a buyer or seller. It is useful to consider the uniqueness of each situation, remembering that what makes these situations alive is that over time everything can change, for example: buyers change preferences; sellers change interests, priorities, pricing; ideas transform; service ebbs and flows; needs and wants evolve; and the competition changes too (Figure 1.1).

Business Development Tip: Clarify If You Are Selling an Inanimate Product or Living People, Ideas, or Services and Manage Buyer Experience Accordingly

The following living sales situations capture most of the situations you will find yourself in at some point in your life, either as a buyer or seller. Find which applies most to your situation and read on.

1. Selling yourself:
   a. for a job;

FIGURE 1.1
Selling in the midst of change.

    b. for a raise;
    c. for a promotion;
    d. for marriage or business partnership.
2. Selling your ideas:
    a. for funding start-ups and new initiatives;
    b. to change the way things are done;
    c. for support of non-profits;
    d. for support of your political, social, economic, or environmental vision of the future;
    e. for peace and a future together.
3. Selling your services:
    a. to members;
    b. as professional service providers.

SELLING YOURSELF FOR A JOB

As MBA professor at Chinese University of Hong Kong and alumni representative for McGill and Bishop's Universities in Canada, I am constantly asked for advice about getting a job. The world has pretty much achieved full employment and robots are picking up the slack. What that means for those without a job is you either "wait for someone to die" (as one of my client organisations referred to their talent management process), become an entrepreneur, or sell yourself into a job by convincing an employer that you are too valuable to ignore. Employers attract, develop, and retain the people they want by, in part, creating jobs for them. If you aren't having success getting a job, you need to boost your sales techniques by using some of the tips and principles outlined in this book. In addition to my tips and principles I also offer the following advice.

In the developed markets of the world today the best candidates speak several languages, have graduated from reputable universities, and are good at what they do. These three attributes however only get you into the running for a job. Competition today for most top jobs is global. How do you get spotted in the crowd amongst so much talent? Employers need to know you, be attracted to what you can offer, and know you fit their budget.

If you are a stranger to your prospective employer, it is impossible for them to know you or know of you. Some job seekers think if they just had the email address for the boss they could send their CV and get the job, but that is not at all how it works. Nowadays, you need to volunteer or work in places where your sought-after employer will get to know you. Employers are hiring their favourite suppliers and clients are hiring consultants whom they have seen in action somewhere else such as the local chamber of commerce or on YouTube. If you don't have a public presence, find out where your relationship target spends their time and put yourself into their sight lines so they can see you in action.

Once your relationship target spots you there are several things you can do to develop the relationship and these are further outlined in the coming pages. To know if you fit their budget you need to do your homework by asking everyone about pay packages and career paths. You don't want to offer yourself cheap because your annual increments start with your entry salary and if it's low, you will be low on the scale for the rest of your career. Similarly, you don't want to ask for too much because it is normal for buyers to like the most expensive items in the shop and then to buy something similar but less expensive. Employers have a budget but so should you, knowing you can travel to a new market and make more money for the same job simply because those skills are in greater demand and shorter supply, pushing up the price of employment accordingly.

Business Development Tip: Do Something to Stand out from the Competition

---

SELLING YOURSELF FOR A RAISE

The most common question I'm asked everywhere in the world is "how do I negotiate for a raise in pay?" The question is normal in that most people feel they are worth more than they are paid and everyone would like to have more money. What everyone asking me this question fails to recognise is that employees are commodities and employers are aiming to maximise their return on investment. That means most employers aren't interested in paying more than they must, nor are they interested in paying more for equivalent service. So how do you sell yourself for a raise? You need to show your employer that you can do more value-added work, either by doing something more important or by doing more of what you have already been doing.

Starting with the latter proposition, since most people are already working 24/7, it is unlikely you will want to do more hours, but many people are willing to work overtime to make more money and sacrifice their personal time in favour of future opportunities for themselves or their families. If this is your situation, then do the calculation and compare the cost of a raise or overtime pay with the cost of hiring another employee. Nowadays, the additional costs and benefits which accompany additional headcount suggests it is cheaper for employers to pay more for their existing employees to produce more output than to hire another employee to help out.

Consider if your employer organisation is growing, shrinking, or stable. If it is growing, they will want to find ways to improve productivity. If it is shrinking, they will want to be cutting costs and headcount. And if it is stable, the attention of employers will be elsewhere.

If you want to ask for a raise in return for doing higher-value work and possibly delegate some of what you are doing to others to free up additional time for the higher-value work then you need to sell yourself for a promotion and ask for a change of title. I address this situation below.

Business Development Tip: Compare Your Cost to the Organisation with the Value You Bring the Organisation

SELLING YOURSELF FOR A PROMOTION

Ambition is both good and bad. On the positive side, it riles against the status quo and allows people to climb the corporate ladder and accomplish things others never thought possible. On the negative side, it can lead to animosity between co-workers or lead people to job-hop without really learning the job or proving their value long term in an organisation.

If you are selling yourself for promotion, it is wise to know that the people who tend to get promoted are the ones who are already performing well in the role they wish to get promoted into. In other words, do your work well, remind people you are doing so, and invite them to consider you for promotion without being hurriedly aggressive.

I had the good fortune of being recruited by Coopers & Lybrand (one of the world's Big Eight accounting firms at that time; there are four now) in my final year of university. I had the requisite attributes they were looking for in new recruits, such as a business degree, eagerness to learn, good interpersonal skills, and proven work experience from part-time jobs. What also differentiated me from the other candidates was that I came to the initial interview with a copy of the firm's published history, *Coopers & Lybrand in Canada: A Chronicle of the McDonald, Currie Years 1010–1973* (Coopers & Lybrand, 1976), which I had read and memorised. Since these books were printed mostly for clients and members of the firm, it was unusual for an interviewee to have one. I had learnt about the book from family connections and asked them if I could read it. Being the only candidate with this book set me apart from the others and was partly what got me my offer letter.

Readers who have worked in big firms know that you can start out as an articling student or apprentice and work your way up to equity partner. If you perform well and people like you, your career can progress quickly up the ranks of the firm with annual promotions. Once you have qualified professionally, you become attractive to clients who like to poach talent from the professional firms to fill internal positions in accounting and finance (for accountants) and in the legal department if you are a lawyer, in real estate if you are an architect, etc.

As you work your way up in any organisation it becomes more of a pyramid than a ladder, meaning each year of promotion will see people leaving the organisation. Some leave because they have found other opportunities they prefer to pursue. Some leave because their performance doesn't warrant promotion and the career track suggests people move either up or out. Some leave because they simply don't like the long hours typical of professional firms where you can get ten years of experience in only five years by working eighty-hour weeks.

People selling themselves for promotion are often stuck into seeing the world only through their own eyes and not from the perspective of the employer. So, if you are looking for promotion, ask yourself: why should your employer promote you? Have you proven to be a leader compared to your colleagues? Have you filled in for more senior people while they were away and proven to excel in higher-level challenges? Do people in the more senior ranks respect and listen to your opinion? Is it time for you to be promoted in the organisation?

A final point of importance that employers look for when selecting leaders is how the candidate has performed in previous roles. To verify performance, employers ask search firms to check references; they speak to your former superiors and they look at your CV to see how long you spent in your previous jobs. In rapidly expanding economies or industries it is relatively easy to get promoted because if your employer holds you back you can try your luck at a competitor. However, this can result in people having worked in five different companies in six years. Good employers shy away from these candidates, realising they never stayed long enough in one job to experience the good or bad impact of their work. Many of these types of candidates leave a trail of destruction behind them because they failed to learn sufficient skills and competencies as they climbed the ladder. People who climb through promotion or job-hopping without gaining the requisite skills and competencies for each new level of challenge and responsibility "rise to the level of their incompetence". This situation was termed *The Peter Principle*, coined by *Dr Lawrence Peter*. If you are selling yourself for promotion, make sure you are ready to perform well at the next level.

Business Development Tip: Ensure Your Seniors Know, Like, and Respect You before Asking Things of Them

SELLING YOURSELF FOR MARRIAGE
OR BUSINESS PARTNERSHIP

Being a friend or co-worker is very different from being a spouse or business partner, but there are also similarities. As traditional marriage vows remind us, marriage (and partnership) is "for better or for worse, till death do us part". While improved healthcare has delayed "death do us part", "for better or for worse" is still a very significant reality in every marriage and business partnership. People wanting to win the hand of another, either in marriage or business partnership, are well advised to spend considerable time in dialogue with their significant other discussing basic values, goals, objectives, how they treat people, their relationship with money, winning and losing, ethics, integrity, and morals. I know these don't sound like topics anyone would like to discuss during their flirtatious courtship phase, but long-term relationship success depends on sufficient common ground in respect of these topics.

Events such as overseas holidays or business launches are mostly always a good time despite being hard work. What is more important is how people react when the going gets tough, as it often does in life and work. Selling your value in situations of stress and crisis and learning how your prospective partner reacts in such circumstances is how you will really see if your future together is sustainable. If you like what you see in each other when the going gets tough then great, but if you don't, avoid signing any agreements. If you see some things you like and some things you don't, ask yourself if you can live with what you don't like, because if not, these are the things that will most likely become the undoing of your marriage or business partnership.

I have many excellent business partnerships but I have also declined several over the years. Thinking of different situations, I have declined or ended business partnerships for the following reasons: breach of trust, theft, differing visions of the future, selfishness, one person doing all the work (me). Meanwhile on the personal front I am still on my first marriage and this is largely because my wife and I can (so far) live with what we dislike about the other while rejoicing in the common ground we share.

A final word on this subject must include experience. I married and entered into (or declined) several business partnerships with a lot less experience than I have now. I encourage you to reach out to friends and mentors to ask for their perspectives before you accept or decline invitations to marriages or business partnerships. It is hard to see things clearly when we lack experience and are emotionally biased. Neutral third parties who care for your best interests and have experience in the situations you are facing, or with the partners you are considering, will give you extremely valuable feedback, if you ask them. If you don't ask them they will still have opinions but will not share them with you, wishing instead for your success and happiness. You must ask.

I was once considering a business partner from the USA and everyone I asked told me they were dishonest and would eventually steal money from me. The American top leadership were incredibly rich and I admired the business they had built around their telco clients globally. Recognising an opportunity for them to bring their services to Asia, I introduced them to one of my clients and made handsome introduction fees for their very sizeable contract which resulted from my introduction. Because of this good beginning I introduced a second successful client and it was here that they stole from me, refusing to pay the introduction fees I was due despite them signing yet another sizeable contract. At this point I ended the relationship and no longer helped them win business in Asia. Today the company no longer exists and the owners further enriched themselves when they sold their business to a large IT company. The moral of the story: ask around, get to know how your prospective partner reacts when the going gets tough, and if you are okay with that then okay; otherwise, move on.

Business Development Tip: Assess Your Partner's Behaviour and Values When They Are Stressed or in Conflict

SELLING YOUR IDEAS FOR FUNDING START-UPS AND NEW INITIATIVES

I have done a lot of Dragon's Den interviews where start-up teams are pitching for support and funding. The best pitches can present their key information in a very short time. The Hong Kong Business Angel Network insists on pitch teams submitting a one-page document for review before they meet any teams. The information they request includes:

- Legal name of the company and key personnel.
- Brief explanation of the market opportunity, niche, target customers, business model, and major milestones.

- Funding needed and use of proceeds.
- Five-year financial projections including sales, cost of goods sold, gross profit, other expenses, and net profit.

The trick to understanding how to sell your start-up idea is to put yourself in the shoes of the investor. Angel investors, venture capitalists, and others in position to vet start-ups all want to pick the best of the best, knowing that on average 90% of start-ups fail but 10% strike it rich. While all start-up ideas are valid, some ideas have a better chance of succeeding than others. The problem with entrepreneurs, especially first-time entrepreneurs, is that they tend to be so enamoured by their idea that they are unable to judge how it compares with other possibilities. If you want to sell your start-up idea, I strongly encourage you to invite a seasoned Dragon's Den judge to look at your one-page pitch summary and provide their assessment. Once you start getting overwhelmingly positive reactions, you know you are onto something. If not, keep reworking your pitch until you too strike gold.

Before leaving the topic of pitching start-ups it is again important to emphasise the importance of your network or ecosystem. It is very different if you are pitching to family and friends in an isolated market or pitching to professional investors in places like Silicon Valley in California or SOSA in Tel Aviv. If your network doesn't include professional investors, ask everyone you know to introduce you to people they know that can help you. Your networking is equally important to your sales pitch because the people you meet along the way will sharpen your thinking and understanding of the market and your prospective start-up.

> **Business Development Tip:** Seek Experienced People to Assess Your Ideas *before* Trying to Sell to Them

SELLING YOUR IDEAS TO CHANGE THE WAY THINGS ARE DONE

One of the first things you learn when working in large organisations is that some things just don't make sense. Processes, methodologies, tools, and people that you find dreadfully outdated are still being used or followed and when you ask why, no one seems to know. There are many reasons why the status quo prevails, including: it works, it's too much trouble to change, no one cares enough to change, it isn't important enough to change, the cost of change exceeds the value of the change, no one knows how to change, no one has ever spotted the opportunity before, no one has the courage to attempt the change, political reasons prevent the change, corruption is involved, it is unclear who is authorised to make the change, etc.

The above list of reasons against change is daunting but change agents aren't slowed by these barriers to change; they simply want to know how to overcome them, sell their ideas, and enact the change they envisage.

All the business development tips quoted above are important but selling change needs more if you want to win. Change leadership requires strategy and strategy requires knowing clearly what you want, who is involved, what the issues are, and how you will manage the time, space, and process of change. Selling your idea is only the beginning of realising change. Even some ideas that get sold never get implemented. The strategy puzzle which I have just referred to is shown below and outlined in greater detail in my book *Dialogue Gap*. I touch upon just three important elements here (Figure 1.2).

The three most important things about selling change include: people, issues, and timing. Identify the people involved and try to classify them as supporters of your change, opponents of your change, and those who either don't care or don't declare their allegiance. In my experience, most change initiatives have 10% of the people in favour of the change, 10% of the people opposing the change, and 80% of the people who sway to the winning side based on political or career objectives. People can be a minefield and if you don't know where people fall with regard to your idea then you need to do your homework. If you don't know where they lie, I suggest you assume them to be opponents and engage them in dialogue to better understand their thinking.

Once you engage people in dialogue about your change ideas you will learn more about the issues involved and importantly how they feel about the issues. Most change initiatives include 50–60 issues and complex change can involve many multiples more. The good news is that issues can be classified into normally 5–8 categories, including issues related to money, people, time, quality, products and services, customers and clients, etc. In my experience, most people who set out to make change happen don't know all the issues. How can you know all the issues? Talk to all the stakeholders and as much as possible talk to experts who have experience with your type of change and who can bring other issues to your attention

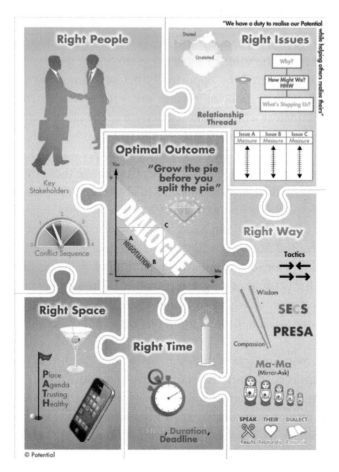

FIGURE 1.2
Dialogue puzzle.

which the stakeholders themselves may not even know exist, for example legal, financial, competitive, etc.

The third very important element of selling change is time. Change agents always want change to move faster and opponents always want change to move more slowly. One of the things you tend to lose with experience is the sense of urgency that accompanies change initiatives. More mature change leaders tend to be satisfied if the direction and momentum of change is aligned with their objectives. Younger leaders, especially freshly minted MBAs, tend to want to see change happen quickly and in so doing alienate several of the stakeholders needed to agree to their change. Slow down if you find speed is creating more resistance than necessary.

Business Development Tip: Use the Dialogue Puzzle to Build Your Strategy for Change

SELLING THE IDEA OF SUPPORT FOR NON-PROFITS

I sit on several not-for-profit boards and advise many not-for-profit organisations. Fundraising and inviting volunteers to support these "third sector" organisations first requires selling the idea of supporting your organisation at all and then, if they are already inclined to support not-for-profit organisations, selling them on the idea of supporting your organisation over others. People have a natural inclination to support organisations that have helped them. It tends to be karma in action or "give and thou shalt receive". The following situations can arise making your sales efforts particularly challenging:

- The person you are wishing to convince is very talented, rich, or networked and everyone is asking them for help.
- The person you are wishing to convince has multiple attachments and they work with their most recent favourites tending to forget those that got them to where they are, for example a person supports their MBA school forgetting their undergraduate university.
- The not-for-profit organisation ignored the target person for decades only to reappear in their lives now that success has allowed the not-for-profit to find them again.
- The person you are wishing to convince has purposely removed themselves from all lists and avoided contact with your not-for-profit either because they had a negative experience, don't want to be asked to give, or feel they have nothing to give.

What to do in these situations? Don't ask them for support until rebuilding relationships. What you learn as you rekindle the relationship will help you understand how this person can help. As you become closer to your target person you will come to know if and how they might want to help your not-for-profit. The trick here is to take the time to rebuild the relationship. Once you think the time is right, you need to ask for their support. During the process of relationship building the keen ones will offer help but with those who resist, you'll need to diagnose why they are resisting. Some people have no time, being pulled in too many directions already by their various personal and professional responsibilities. Some must be protective of their high-level relationships because if they start referring you they will lose their friends. Some have quite different plans for their money or share their money with others, for example, a family business where others in the family are not interested in giving to your not-for-profit.

Another problem which might be stifling your not-for-profit is that your target person is put off by some of the people on the board of your not-for-profit. It is important to continuously renew board membership to prevent calcification, causing a lack of openness to new ideas, ways of being, and ways of doing. One experienced board member, when asked what she does with "dead wood" on her board, said she tells people explicitly to "either give us your money, share your network, use your skills, or get out of the way".

Business Development Tip: Rekindle Relationships *before* Asking for Support

SELLING YOUR POLITICAL, SOCIAL, ECONOMIC, OR ENVIRONMENTAL VISION OF THE FUTURE

The world is polarised at this moment in history because our shared planet is giving an uneven reality to its inhabitants. Some consume vastly more goods and services than others, some experience pollution far worse than others, some live in far superior conditions than others, some overeat while others starve, some enjoy the best healthcare while others have none, and some are infinitely richer than others. All these discrepancies are causing people around the world to mobilise groups locally and over the internet to rally for their cause. Unfortunately, no one seems intent on listening to the other, so passionate advocates are burning out and becoming apathetic because of their inability to sell their vision of the future to others.

Successful advocacy groups today leverage all the resources available to win their campaign. Resources such as slick branding and marketing, use of social media, focused sales efforts with high-level thought leaders, sustained effort over time, and emotionally grabbing appeals. Of course, all of this takes money and winning advocacy groups have money too, having lined this up before setting out to change the world.

What is the lesson for you wanting to sell your ideas for support of your political, social, economic, or environmental vision of the future today? The competition today is rich and shrewd and you need to be equally or better prepared than the competition. When I think how the big socio-political trends of the nineteenth century spread across Europe and Asia I realise how much more difficult it would be for this to happen today, where competing sides like the Republicans and Democrats in the USA are equally well resourced to sell their particular vision of the future.

A final comment on this topic must address the political. I have always aimed for the optimal outcome as defined by Nobel Prize-winning economist John Nash, who proved that the optimal outcome is the point at which no one party can benefit further without another party losing something. Achieving optimal outcomes requires dialogue and negotiation amongst all key stakeholders but if one party is holding out for the party line instead of the optimal outcome, as appears to be the case with public healthcare in the USA, then politics prevents the sale of optimal ideas. Ask yourself in your situation what role politics is playing, if any, in preventing your ability to sell your vision of the future. When politics confronts environment we all lose, because politicians that don't protect the environment for political reasons cause all of us to suffer negative outcomes. It is one thing to put politics ahead of economic good but putting politics ahead of environment is deadly.

Business Development Tip: How Are Politics Preventing Your Selling an Optimal Solution in Your Situation?

SELLING YOUR IDEAS FOR PEACE AND A FUTURE TOGETHER

My dialogue and negotiation work has given me the opportunity to advise some of the most intractable conflicts in the world, including Israel–Palestine, Iran–USA–Saudi Arabia, China–Tibet–Taiwan, North–South Korea, Quebec–Canada, and Hong Kong–China. While these situations garner a lot of interest, my work more often covers conflict situations common to sales, procurement, service, change management, leadership, government, environment, etc. My work has even extended into personal conflicts such as family business and divorce.

In all these situations people are struggling to sell their ideas for peace and, if not a future together, at least a future where all stakeholders can live peaceably. What prevents people from selling their ideas in these situations? A lot of the issues preventing resolution are emotional and not always rational. When people have suffered repeatedly over time they tend to lose hope or care for a future together. Some become revengeful and do all they can to attack the other. In situations that have experienced hostility it takes a long time for things to settle, if they ever do. This is equally true in labour disputes, family disputes, and international disputes. *Leaders must do all they can to prevent hostilities from erupting, by choosing dialogue over conflict.*

Further advice for a peaceful future together includes: spend all the time required to understand the other side, attempting as much as possible to find reasons to have compassion for them and their situation. In doing so you will better understand where they are coming from, why they are so intransigent, and what you will need to adjust to sell your idea of the future. Taking the time to fully understand the other may also help you realise that your hope for a future together is not to be realised in your lifetime and that you are better off separating, changing employer, moving away, or doing whatever your conflict situation might warrant to give you a better future.

I was once amongst a small group of very successful representatives for another person's business. When the owner's business partner retired, we all believed it was time for the remaining partner to share equity and grow the business. The surviving owner didn't agree and after exhaustive talks we realised there was no changing his mind, so we all departed the organisation. It wasn't an optimal situation, but I wasn't prepared to spend years waiting for the owner to change his mind. Twenty years later the owner asked me if I wanted to buy his business.

French nationalists began agitating in the 1960s for reduced English influence in the Province of Quebec in Canada. Although the English had conquered the French in an epic battle that ceded Lower Canada to the British Empire hundreds of years earlier, demographics meant that French speakers vastly outnumbered English speakers in the

City of Montreal where I was born and by the time I graduated from university the political upheavals caused by Quebec separatism meant it would take a few generations for the economy to recover, if ever it would. Not wanting to wait around I began my international career as soon as possible and have lived abroad ever since. The Quebec separatists understood their economy would take a hit in return for achieving their political aims. What separatists failed to foresee was that French young people, like young people everywhere, want jobs and opportunities and as the world globalised, Quebec became a backwater, shedding jobs and forcing talent of all languages to migrate to other parts of Canada and beyond.

In both examples above the stakeholders failed to fully recognise the needs of both the organisation and the individuals involved. By disregarding the individual needs, the target persons failed to achieve their objectives. Both the consultancy and the province failed to retain their talent.

Business Development Tip: Sell Your Ideas to Both the Organisation and the Individual You Are Targeting

SELLING YOUR SERVICES TO MEMBERS

The internet has been a disrupter for a lot of industries. Membership-based groups have been almost as affected by the internet as publishing, music, movies, and postal services. Prior to the arrival of the internet the only way you could easily connect with like-minded people was to join a group. "Member since 19xx" carried an amount of respect. If you were a member of a private club, this gave you a direct connection to persons of influence for business and politics. Being a member of exclusive clubs still carries the weight it did before but open membership groups such as chambers of commerce and less exclusive sports and social clubs have all haemorrhaged members if they defined their value proposition solely based on being a part of their membership directory. The groups that have survived and thrived know all their members personally and work hard to provide value in the form of introductions, membership discounts, member services not easily acquired elsewhere, reciprocal arrangements with other similar member groups, business development assistance, supplier referrals, etc.

Given the rather dramatic change in the landscape, many membership groups (like chambers of commerce and golf clubs) have shrunk or closed while others (like Uber and Costco) have sprung up and flourished. What is the secret of membership groups today that successfully sell to their members? They know what the members want and they give it to them. How do they know what their members want? They dialogue with them and ask. How do they deliver value to members? They brainstorm ways to help, pilot ideas, and expand the ideas that show success with members. It isn't like before where member clubs could simply ask members to cover deficits at the end of the month through supplementary dues. Nowadays, if you aren't delivering value, be it industry groups, professional groups, social groups, sports groups, or even personal groups, your members will quit and go elsewhere.

I was a member of several chambers of commerce in Hong Kong when the global financial crisis hit and forced a review of expenses. At the time, I was a member of roughly a dozen membership groups and none were bringing value. I cancelled all but one membership. The one membership I kept was with an organisation I was helping strategise a new direction for members. One of the problems with this organisation was that the leadership changed annually and had little regard for members, preferring instead to use their leadership roles in this organisation to self-aggrandise their professional image. I sat with the organisation's director of business development, taught him how to use our value proposition template (explained in Chapter 2) to voice out what they could do for me, and asked once they could demonstrate value for me I would re-join. To this day the organisation has been unable to demonstrate their value proposition and they have become a shell of their former selves.

The moral of this story is that even if you can demonstrate value to members, be sure your organisation leadership isn't intervening to ruin your sales efforts. Until everyone is aligned and on board, isolated sales efforts can bring small results at best.

Business Development Tip: Align Leadership and Sales to Prove Value to Members

SELLING PROFESSIONAL SERVICES

It is not by chance that selling professional services is introduced after having learnt all the other types of selling outlined above. This is because selling professional services is the bread and butter for most people in developed economies where services outsell products in terms of gross domestic product (Figure 1.3). Buying professional services also tends to be expensive and if things go wrong clients are left both out of pocket and very negatively affected. One needs only think of lawyers who lose their client's case, doctors sued for medical negligence, engineers and architects who make mistakes, or auditors that misstate assets or liabilities.

FIGURE 1.3
Pyramid.

Selling professional services is a live activity amidst constant change. Getting the process right ensures sufficient feedback loops to accommodate change and quality control at the same time (Appendix VII).

Business Development Tip: Follow the DIALOGUE Sales Process to Improve Results

I credit my dialogue sales process to working with JP Morgan in Japan. They seemed receptive to understanding the process step by step and this was the first chance I got to spell things out in terms of a flowchart. Actual sales seldom flow start to finish and instead you pick up the flow someplace through the process but in almost every case good service selling will follow the process as laid out. I will outline this process in the following chapter.

2

The Dialogue Selling Process

In every sales situation, there is both a seller and a buyer and, like two figure skaters on ice, at different times either the buyer or the seller may take the lead. The dance they perform together may or may not lead to a deal, but it will leave them knowing a little more about each other's strengths and weaknesses. What I observed as I studied business development was that these two dancers are connected and follow the same steps as they dance together. The five steps they follow are to plan, connect, dialogue, record, and follow up. The five steps became the basis of the dialogue process which I outline in this chapter and the image I use to represent this is the DNA module, the basis of all life where one outer band is the seller, the other the buyer, and the five bars connecting the two are the five steps they perform over and over as they twirl around the ice or dance floor in the process of buying and selling. Once they complete the five steps, the dance repeats as shown in Figure 1.4.

PLAN – EARN THE RIGHT TO DISCUSS CLIENT NEEDS

Plan refers to what sellers (and buyers) must do before meeting their respective dance partner. The first thing at this stage is to earn the right to discuss client needs. Dancers and skaters hit the gym, study choreography, choose a club or studio, select their costumes, and then aim to dance with a partner. Professional service sellers need to become experts in their own right and do what is needed to make themselves attractive before setting out to meet and connect with prospective buyers. In your specific situation, this might mean becoming an international lawyer, accountant, or banker with years of relevant experience before you have the right to meet a prospective buyer. High-level buyers aren't looking to dance with just anyone; they too have a choice and are looking for the qualifications, experience and pedigree that warrants the situation requiring investment on their part.

In most situations, earning the right to discuss client needs involves garnering ten or more years of work experience, during which time you build your bio and an impressive client list, become able to afford to live and work where the buyers reside, and rise to be amongst the best in your industry. A lot of young people lack patience and wish to buy the right to discuss client needs sooner, either by completing a higher-level degree or investing in branding and sales. The problem with trying to rush the process is that once you are in position but lack experience, you inevitably make mistakes before you pick up the things you missed through lack of experience.

I am grateful to have had the chance to work with Dr Robert Fung, who, before he passed away, was the most experienced paediatrician in Hong Kong. Robert was referred repeatedly for cases that less experienced paediatricians could not diagnose. With his professional experience and superior attention skills, he would sit with the child and mother in his office and almost always figure out what the problem was. Robert had earned the right to be referred the most challenging cases in Hong Kong by studying sufficiently to attend and graduate from McGill University's world-renowned School of Medicine, then working and staying up to date in his profession for over 20 years while he built his practice.

It is not by spending excessive amounts of money buying degrees from top ranked universities that you earn the right to discuss clients' needs. Like pilots that are promoted to commercial airline captains, only after they have put in the years and personally experienced all of what can happen (good and bad) when piloting aircraft, have they earned the right to look after the lives of hundreds of people in aircrafts costing hundreds of millions of dollars.

The good news is buyers, like sellers, also rank in terms of scale and importance. You gain experience selling by starting out with relatively smaller and less significant situations and then, bit by bit, as your experience grows, so too will the size and significance of your accounts. The following pages will guide you through the dance with your prospective buyers as you rise in importance to the top of your industry. It isn't getting older that will get you to the top; you need to get better too. This process will help you get better each step of the dance.

Business Development Tip: Don't Sell Yourself, Your Ideas, or Your Services Until You Have Earned the Right by Gaining the Skills and Experience Buyers Want to Buy

PLAN – MAP YOUR NETWORK

Launching a professional services business requires many things but, since it is all about relationships, one of the first things you need to do is take a piece of paper and begin mapping your network. You can map your network using mind mapping, radials (as shown below), or simple spreadsheets. The goals of network mapping include identifying your key relationships in each category and assessing the strength of your relationship threads (how well you know each other) with each of your key relationships. Let me begin by explaining how I map my network to give you an example to follow. I suggest you begin with a paper and pencil and, once your categorisation makes sense, you can then add the names of the people and organisations to your map. Your categories may differ slightly from mine depending upon your situation.

Business Development Tip: Map Your Network Overview to Identify Strengths and Weaknesses

PETER NIXON NETWORK MAP – OVERVIEW

Figure 2.1 shows an overview of the Peter Nixon Network Map.

PETER NIXON NETWORK MAP – CLIENTS BY EXPERTISE

Each of the above shapes can be further defined before identifying the individual relationships in each category. I show below two ways to sub-divide my client category before drilling down one further level where I identify specific people and organisations. If you are using mind mapping for this exercise, these sub-categories would be smaller branches coming out of the original branches (Figure 2.2).

FIGURE 2.1
PAN network – overview.

FIGURE 2.2
PAN network by client expertise.

> **Business Development Tip:** Map Your Network by Expertise to Identify Strengths and Weaknesses

PETER NIXON NETWORK MAP – CLIENTS BY GEOGRAPHIC AREA

Figure 2.3 shows the PAN network by geography.

> **Business Development Tip:** Map Your Network by Geography to Identify Strengths and Weaknesses

PETER NIXON NETWORK MAP – CLIENTS IN APAC – BY SECTOR

Figure 2.4 shows the PAN network of APAC clients by sector.

FIGURE 2.3
PAN network by geography.

FIGURE 2.4
PAN network APAC clients by sector.

> **Business Development Tip:** Map Your Network by Sector to Identify Strengths and Weaknesses

PETER NIXON NETWORK MAP – CLIENTS IN APAC – PRIVATE SECTOR

The next level of your network map is where you identify the specific organisations you work with (if you have a small number of clients you can skip this level and proceed directly to the last level) (Figure 2.5).

> **Business Development Tip:** Map Your Network by Sub-Sector to Identify Strengths and Weaknesses

PETER NIXON NETWORK MAP – CLIENTS IN APAC – PRIVATE SECTOR – CLIENT A

Figure 2.6 shows several different people I know at Client A. The different lines represent the strength of the relationship threads with each

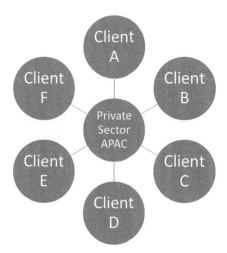

FIGURE 2.5
PAN network APAC private sector.

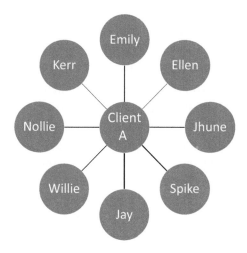

FIGURE 2.6
PAN network client A (APAC Private sector).

individual. I discuss relationship threads later in this chapter and, at this stage, all that you need to understand is that the more solid the line, the stronger the relationship threads we have binding our relationships. As shown in the chart, I know Jay and Spike better than the others and I know the two girls, Kerr and Ellen, the least. People I don't really know, other than to say hello, are not shown in the network map because I don't know them very well at all. Selling yourself, your ideas, or your services to people you don't know well is near impossible.

Business Development Tip: Map Your Network by Client to Identify Strengths and Weaknesses

Don't spend too much time mapping your network because you'll never actually sell anything unless you are in dialogue with clients and prospective clients. Maps are good to have but dialogues are essential.

PLAN – COMPLETE THE BUSINESS DEVELOPMENT ROADMAP

My Business Development Roadmap ("Roadmap") was created to help people knowing nothing about sales but wondering what they needed to do, who they needed to sell to, what was preventing them from selling, how they planned to overcome the barriers preventing them from selling, and who they would ask to help them overcome their barriers to selling. My Roadmap is included in the Appendix.

The Roadmap focuses on what is most important for service professionals making the jump into business development. Most professionals will look for every reason to avoid selling because they simply prefer other activities and that is why they became lawyers, bankers, accountants, etc. in the first place. By focusing your attention on who you should be talking to, and then asking yourself why you aren't doing so, you are staring at the problem. By purposely seeking out people to help you overcome your self-imposed barriers to success (e.g. business development coaches), you are simply recognising that if you could do it yourself, you already would have and, since you can't, you need help.

Sales result from dialogue. During the height of the global financial crisis, on a weekday mid-afternoon in a coffee shop far from his office, I unexpectedly ran into a partner from one of the law firms that I had worked with not long before. I asked what he was up to and he said it was dead quiet in the markets and his phone hadn't rung in weeks, so he was taking time away from the office to read some leisure books and spend time with family. I value reading and family time, but I also know that sitting in the office waiting for the phone to ring, or replacing business development with hobbies and family time, isn't going to help you develop your business.

It is important to use the quiet periods between engagements to get busy with business development. Taking a passive approach and waiting for the phone to ring isn't going to make you successful. Despite this, avoiding sales dialogues is typical of a lot of service professionals.

Business Development Tip: Identify What is Preventing You from Doing Business Development and Who Will Help You Change Your Behaviour

CONNECT – DEVELOP SECS APPEAL

Malcolm Gladwell, in his book entitled *The Tipping Point: How Little Things Can Make a Big Difference* (Abacus, 2000), shares stories of successful networkers and identifies four traits that successful networkers have in common. Gladwell refers to these four traits with the acronym "CESS". I simply reorder these to make them more memorable and refer to them as "SECS Appeal". The four traits include the following:

Sociable – To sell well, you need to be the one who proactively connects with other people, either in person or by telephone. It is normal for natural salespeople to want to do this, but for most service professionals this is hard work because service professionals (in my experience) tend to be less comfortable inquisitively conversing with others, especially strangers. Being less willing and comfortable to socialise simply means you need to make the effort when it is necessary and build gaps into your day to catch up without people around you. It isn't always easy, but it is always valuable.

Business Development Tip: Avoid Business Development Until You Are Willing to Be Sociable

Energetic – The term "rainmaker" refers to indigenous North Americans that are so talented they can even make it rain. This term is used in professional services selling to refer to people able to win business anywhere. Apart from being sociable, rainmakers are also energetic and, through eye contact, a wide smile, active body language, engaging conversation, and activity, they energise the people around them. If you don't see this behaviour as describing you and think if you don't have it you can't do business development, that's not correct. Everyone has things or people they are passionate about and when you talk about these topics your energy explodes. The secret of SECS Appeal is finding and using these topics as your internal energy pack.

Business Development Tip: Avoid Business Development until You Have the Energy to be Outgoing

Curiosity – I have a natural curiosity to know everyone I meet. I believe everyone has a uniqueness to them and something of value to share with the world, which is of benefit if I can discover it, but the challenge of course is finding out what it is. This is where good business development professionals excel, because they are curious. In my work, I have the good fortune of meeting thousands of people and everyone gives me something of value. Some help me see things from a different perspective. Some help me realise I can help in a different way. Some teach me. Some refer me. Some make me laugh. Some make me more compassionate. Some leave me puzzled. I could go on, but in the short time I have with most people I meet, I genuinely try to find this nugget. Be curious but don't interrogate others. When I was young I asked too many questions of my grandmother's friend from Europe. I was curious about her World War II experience but my curiosity (and youthful ignorance of history) offended her and she asked that I stop asking questions. I recommend asking as much as you can but also being alert when your questions become overly inquisitive. I recently asked a taxi driver about his family in Iran and he went silent then said he had no family. I changed the subject, knowing migrants everywhere leave behind family and do not always want to talk about it except with their closest friends. I'm still learning how to balance my natural curiosity with being overly inquisitive. If you have to err on one side or the other, I recommend asking as many questions as you can. The more you know, the more you win.

Business Development Tip: Avoid Business Development until You Are Ready to Talk about Them Instead of Yourself

Self-Confident – The fourth trait of successful networkers is self-confidence. This again isn't an issue until you either overdo it and look cocky or feel it lacking and look unconvincing. If you are going to sell yourself, your ideas, or your services to other people, you must look like you believe in what you are saying. At the heart of looking convincing is showing confidence. Self-confidence comes across in the way you speak, what you say, how you sit or stand, and how you dress. One valuable lesson I learnt was from my voice coach at the Hong Kong Academy for Performing Arts. My voice coach was an older gentleman from the UK who taught Italian opera and looked and sounded the part. There is something about being a global expert that enables you to walk and talk with confidence, but for the rest of us still aiming to build our expertise or facing situations new to us, it is useful to know a few stage tricks. Stand up and imagine I am holding a big block of ice between your shoulder blades. What would you do? The normal reaction is to gasp a big breath of air due to the cold and to thrust your shoulders back and your chest forward. This puts you in a position of self-confidence and your deep breath will give you a stronger voice. The second trick my voice coach taught me was to slow down my speech, move my mouth fully, and pronounce every vowel with exaggeration. For example, moving your mouth fully to pronounce the vowels, say ex-agg-er-a-tion. Practise using different words for a minute or two and, after you finish, you will notice that your regular speech has slowed, your pronunciation has improved, and your appearance of confidence is better than before.

Business Development Tip: Learn to Show Self-Confidence to Improve Your Business Development

CONNECT – THE MAGIC OF HUMAN RELATIONSHIPS

I recognise three magic aspects in human relationships. The first is that we naturally want to help the people we know. The second is that every relationship can bring you value in some way (e.g. friendship, referrals, business, or help). Third is that everyone suffers in some way and by being compassionate and helping others they will want to help you. The magic of relationships means the more people you know the easier it is for you to do business development. Below I discuss the five categories of relationships which you should focus on to improve your business development results.

CONNECT – CONTACT STALE RELATIONSHIPS

You normally feel special when contacted by old friends (although it is natural to know some people you don't want to see again). We grow apart from old friends and make new ones as our lives change. Whenever we change jobs, have children, move to a new home, change hobbies, travel, etc., we open to new relationships but given the finite amount of time available for staying in touch it is natural some relationships go stale over time. Since the people you have known will still want to help you if they know how, it is valuable to keep in touch. A good way to do so is to reconnect with old friends via social media, for example, recognise their birthdays, send greetings for Christmas or New Year's, etc. All you need to tell them is that you still care for them, what specifically you are doing now, and how they can reach you if they want to stay in touch. Here is an example:

> Dear Natacha, we haven't been in touch for years but we found you on Facebook, we miss you and we hope all is well. I am now a negotiation consultant (www.potentialdialogue.com) and Marie is a parenting consultant (www.parentingdialogue.com). Send us news if you can. We hope all is well. Best regards, Peter.

Business Development Tip: Keep in Touch with Everyone You Know at Least Once a Year

CONNECT – CONTACT EXISTING CLIENTS AT LEAST THREE TIMES PER YEAR

It is normal that you contact your clients at least once a year for business reasons, for example, annual tax filing, annual physical, or annual visit to the dentist or eye doctor. Successful business development professionals recognise that if you contact your clients a few other times during the year, they will either welcome your approach or not. Many of us dislike product salespeople who keep contacting us because we find this intrusive. The secret of successful relationship selling is following your relationship threads to stay in touch.

I explain relationship threads separately but, at this stage, all you need to remember is to stay in touch with stale relationships (you care, what you are doing now, how to reach you) but, in addition to this, you attach something you know they will find interesting because you know they like this, for example, a business subject, a personal hobby, someone you know in common, etc. I call these relationship threads and they create "non-sales opportunities to stay in touch". More on this later.

Business Development Tip: Keep in Touch with Clients More Often Than They Expect

CONNECT – NETWORK IN DIVERSE GROUPS

It is impossible to discover new things if you hang out all the time with the same people. To open yourself to new ideas, new perspectives, new people, and new opportunities, you should network in a wide variety of groups. For example, when I worked as an auditor, I spent all my time with work colleagues and clients. Since I worked such long hours, my colleagues were also my friends and social time seldom opened to other people. When I married, my network widened to include my wife's friends and family. These new people in my life brought new opportunities. When we had children, the families of our children's friends also widened our circle of contacts. When I began my business, I had to purposefully spend less time with old colleagues to create new windows of time to spend meeting new contacts. I found this difficult, but I quickly realised the importance of prospective clients. I joined chambers of commerce and various industry and interest groups to purposefully network with more diverse people. In doing so, I met new friends, competitors, clients, and suppliers. I stayed in touch with my old colleagues but suddenly my address book swelled from a few dozen contacts to a few hundred.

Business Development Tip: Network in Diverse Groups to Uncover New Opportunities

CONNECT – NETWORK INTERNALLY

People do business with people they know and like. If you have developed a successful relationship with someone needing services you can't provide personally, is it common for people in large firms to overlook internal colleagues and instead refer work to friends in other firms. If you work in a large firm and have several years' experience, this won't come as a surprise. To others however this must appear crazy. The main challenge in large firms is that everyone is busy and it is common to spend little if any time networking internally. Even when there is an internal networking opportunity, for example, an annual dinner, colleagues sit with friends and there is little mixing between different teams or divisions.

To overcome this challenge, you should do two things: purposely network with others outside your immediate team, and when you do network, for example, lunch or coffee together, share examples of your work in a way your colleagues understand and can refer you when they hear of similar situations arising in their client base. The best way to share experience is by using a common template. The template I use is called the Value Proposition Template, described separately herein.

> **Business Development Tip:** Network Internally so Your Colleagues Know You, Know What You Do, and Can Refer You

CONNECT – NETWORK – USE SOCIAL MEDIA TO CONNECT TO YOUR NETWORK AT LEAST ONCE A DAY IF NOT MORE OFTEN

Social media has basically divided the market into two halves: those who use it and those who don't. The line isn't a straight one, but in my experience, it does a pretty good job of dividing people into young and old, global and local, open and closed to change. I accept all the arguments about both the good and bad effects imposed upon society by social media, but the fact is at this point in history it is a very big thing and there is no indication it will be going away. As a result, people unwilling to leverage its power are missing its usefulness for growing and strengthening their network of relationships. Likewise, if you over rely on the internet and avoid face-to-face real-time relationships, you will hurt your relationship building efforts. We can all think of people who to us seem very interesting on social media but then leave you disinterested in person.

There exists a vast and growing list of possibilities for you to leverage social media to grow and strengthen your relationships. If you are like me, because people have app preferences, you probably stay in touch with different people on different apps. Other writers can fill you in on how and when to use the various social media currently available. I wish to remind readers that if you are not using social media at all, or only in a limited way to further your business development efforts, then you are missing significant opportunities. Hire a young tech-savvy social media expert and put them in charge of posting regular messages to targeted groups, reminding the world about your value, your ideas, and your services. What to post I address below, and the questions of where and how often depend on your web strategy. One thing to remember is the need today to be posting often enough that your target audience will see at least one of your messages amongst the thousands they receive daily.

Before leaving the topic of social media, some readers might be wondering if email is still valid, and the answer is yes. Some of your target audience (and many of the most important buyers) are still predominantly email users. Leverage messaging apps, such as Constant Contact and others which enable you to send emails to your address book, while also sharing these on LinkedIn, Facebook, Twitter, etc.

Business Development Tip: Use Social Media to Connect with Your Network Daily

CONNECT – INTRODUCE YOURSELF

The first step in building relationships is introducing yourself. Of course, you can talk to strangers without introductions but if you want to develop lasting relationships, the sooner and better your introduction is made, the more likelihood of a good start in your relationship. Since first impressions are so important, getting off to a good start is VERY important, especially with people you are targeting as being important for some reason in your life, for example, friends, referrals, help, business. There are five things that your introduction should cover. The information should not all come out at the same time (this puts people off), but before saying goodbye to your target person they should know your name, how to contact you, and be clear on the following:

- Who are you (something personal)? E.g. father of three children.
- What is your expertise? E.g. international adviser for people facing tough negotiations.
- Where did you learn your expertise/get experience? E.g. Big Four accounting firm international experience, public and private sector clients around the world.
- What quantifiable VALUE do you bring? E.g. $/quality/time – see value proposition examples below.
- Who are some of your clients or what are some of your signature projects? Governments A, B, C, Companies D, E, F, Projects G, H, I, etc.

How you introduce yourself is as important as what you say. Here are six tips to improve the chances people become interested to know more.

1. *Don't say everything at once.* Normally, when you introduce yourself, you want to leave time for the other person to introduce themselves as well. It is very unlikely they will remember much of what you say. Just think how often you forget the name of the person you have just met. If they can't remember your name, they certainly won't remember much of what you say afterwards until something catches their full attention and they tune into what you are saying 100%. Be sure you have their full attention and interest before proceeding with more of your introduction.

2. *Be humble and kind.* No one likes rude or boastful people and if you have already been lucky enough to develop some fame, others may know more about you than you think. This is especially true today now that people can check you out on the internet moments before meeting you. Simply stating some of your signature clients and projects should be enough to underline your expertise. Being kind and compassionate will always be better than being dismissing, critical, rude. You never know what doors open or close to you in those few moments when meeting new people.

3. *Smile and use humour.* People naturally gravitate towards people they feel comfortable with and if you can break the ice by smiling and being somewhat light-hearted (self-deprecating humour is good) then you are bound to find relationships starting off on the right foot. There will always be time to get serious once you know each other.

4. *Choose words to connect.* Do your best to choose words, examples, and dialect, which the other person can relate to easily. If I am talking to an engineer, I'll refer to my engineering related client work. If I'm talking to a banker, I'll relate banking client examples. I'll try to use a few words in their first language to demonstrate a little of my experience in their country or culture. I'll try to identify their motivational dialect and use words which motivate them, e.g. I'll use more personal language for relationship style persons and more rationale language for more learned persons.

5. *Be clear.* Possibly most important of all is to speak clearly and loud enough for them to hear you. We often meet people for the first time in social settings where it is noisy and harder to hear what people are saying. Don't let your introduction go unheard. In Asia, it is normal to exchange business cards and spend time on the card details before proceeding. This helps clarity but if the name you wish to be referred to doesn't stand out on your card then tell them to call you by the name you wish.

6. *Demonstrate your SECS Appeal.* As explained earlier, be sure your introduction includes self-confidence, energy, curiosity, and sociability. Missing any of these will diminish your chances of success.

If you are lucky enough to be introduced by a mutual friend, or if you find yourself making introductions between two of your contacts, be sure your introductions include all the above details as well as how you know each of the people you are introducing. If your introducer hasn't explained how you know each other then take a moment to explain this and ask the other person to do the same. Doing so creates a nice relationship thread before proceeding. In this way, your friend's friends can become your friends.

Business Development Tip: Introduce Yourself and Others Effectively

CONNECT – SHARE YOUR VALUE PROPOSITIONS AS APPROPRIATE

Value propositions are straightforward, easy-to-grasp examples of the value you offer clients. To become fluent at identifying and sharing these examples, it is useful to use my value proposition template to ensure each example includes the key information in the right sequence. Once the value propositions are written they become easy to share with others including people you know (such as colleagues, friends, and employees) who can voice them out on your behalf. I set out the template below and then provide a few examples.

BLANK VALUE PROPOSITION TEMPLATE

As a result of who _____

_____

doing what _____

when _____

the target audience _____

benefitted by (or will benefit by) (quantified value created)

_____

_____

leading to (next step) _____

VALUE PROPOSITION TEMPLATE – NEGOTIATION EXAMPLE

As a result of my negotiation training for the distressed debt team of a large UK bank in the aftermath of the Asian Financial Crisis, the team was able to recover hundreds of millions of dollars more than they had been offered, resulting in the bank extending my training to include their procurement teams globally, the savings of which were equivalent to the bank's net profit annually for several years.

VALUE PROPOSITION TEMPLATE – DIALOGUE EXAMPLE

As a result of my training in dialogue methods for managers and partners of a large international audit firm, the target audience were able to improve dialogue with existing client accounts, resulting in such noticeably improved results* that the firm employed me and two of my colleagues to train all their managers and partners across Asia. (*Client declined my request to disclose increased fees but said it was significant.)

VALUE PROPOSITION TEMPLATE – CONFLICT EXAMPLE

As a result of my coaching a client continuously during a three-year period, he was able to productively overcome the sudden termination of an important business relationship without losing millions of dollars, status in the industry, or self-esteem, allowing him to launch a new venture internationally, which today brings him more value than he risked losing when first notified of his termination.

VALUE PROPOSITION TEMPLATE – CHARITY SUPPORT

As a result of donors giving unwanted jewellery to a food charity for sale at their annual glamour event, the charity was able to raise several hundred thousands of dollars, enabling them to feed hundreds of kids every morning at school, resulting in improved attention, better grades, and continuation to higher learning.

Business Development Tip: Write and Share Your Value Proposition

DIALOGUE – CHANGE YOUR DIALECT TO CONNECT WITH AND INFLUENCE OTHERS

In my books on negotiation and dialogue, I take some time to introduce and explain the concept of motivational dialect (Appendix IX). Readers interested in learning more about this important topic are encouraged to read those books. The concept is a simple one. People are primarily motivated by either: results, relationships, or rationale. If you find yourself talking to someone who appears to be results-oriented, emphasise the results that can be achieved if they follow you, your ideas, or hire your services. If they are more relationship oriented, then emphasise the people they know with whom you have worked and how much they have enjoyed it. If they are more rationale-oriented then emphasise your academic background, the logic of your ideas, or the validity of your services. Here is an example of someone selling to three different people, each motivated by something quite different than the other. Key words are shown in italics.

- Results: "I'd like to share with you the *improved sales* our clients have achieved because of following our dialogue selling process. Apart from *20% improvement in turnover*, key accounts are reporting *better supplier satisfaction* and *reduced attrition*".
- Relationships: "I'd like to share with you the *greatly enhanced relationships* our clients have been able to achieve by following our dialogue selling process. *Supplier satisfaction* survey results are up, *attrition is down*, and we have even increased sales by 20%".
- Rationale: "I'd like to share with you the *thinking behind our dialogue selling process*. By following a *logical process* to create, strengthen, and maintain relationships, *client research shows* improved sales, satisfaction, and reduced attrition".

Business Development Tip: Change Your Dialect to Connect with and Influence Others

DIALOGUE – ASK QUESTIONS (BRING MA-MA TO THE TABLE)

Over the years, I have had all sorts of jobs where questioning was at the very heart of my work. Counselling, journalism, auditing, coaching, consulting, training; all require knowing how to ask questions well. I've learnt active listening, reflective questions, appreciative inquiry, and more. According to people that have taken my courses, one of the most memorable things in all of what I teach is my questioning technique, which I called Ma-Ma. I call it Ma-Ma for three very important reasons.

Firstly, everyone who has ever experienced a mother's love has also witnessed how, in their typically maternal way, they put aside everything and focus on their child. The mother then mirrors the emotion the child is emitting and asks questions to find out what has happened and how they feel, not stopping until they have diagnosed the situation and proceeded to a solution. This is exactly the behaviour I encourage you to demonstrate when you are in dialogue with others, regardless of whether you are selling, negotiating, or conversing. Put aside what you are doing, focus 100% on the other party, mirror what they say and how they feel, and ask questions to diagnose the situation and possible solutions.

Secondly Ma-Ma is an acronym for mirror-ask, mirror-ask. In other words, it reminds you to mirror the words and emotions of the person you are in dialogue with and then to ask a question to go deeper into the subject they are sharing with you. Since Ma-Ma suggests doing this twice, it also reminds you not to change topic but to continue to probe deeper into the subject at hand. I encourage you to ask five times, mirroring each time you go, delving deeper and deeper into understanding the reasons underlying what the other party initially expressed by you. The Ma-Ma technique is like peeling an onion where each layer reveals a better understanding of what is really going on. In Asia, where culture dictates not sharing emotions as much as, say, Latin cultures, I have found the Ma-Ma technique incredibly useful. I have also found the Ma-Ma technique incredibly useful in American culture where people might appear very friendly but seldom inquire beyond superficial topics, believing that if it is important, people will talk about it anyway. This same behaviour can be generalised to males who, in my experience, will speak less often in depth when compared with women.

Thirdly the Ma-Ma technique allows for me to say, "Bring Ma-Ma to the table", which seems to be enough for the thousands of people who have attended my training courses to realise it isn't until they stop making statements and start asking questions that they will be able to break a deadlock, diagnose a situation, get to know the person in front of them, test out possible solutions, etc. In all your dialogues, I therefore encourage you to bring Ma-Ma to the table.

The Ma-Ma technique, although based on a mother's love for her child, doesn't necessarily mean Ma-Ma comes more naturally to a woman than a man. I know several women who struggle with this technique and I know several men who are natural wonders at focusing on others instead of themselves, and asking questions about others' needs and wants.

The four main problems experienced by people trying to learn the Ma-Ma technique include:

1. *Thinking too much* about what you are going to ask instead of simply listening deeply to the other person, mirroring what they say or feel, and then asking an open question about what they said. You don't need to prepare. You need to be 100% present and listen;
2. *Not mirroring before asking* questions, making it sound more like an interrogation. Mirroring is needed to validate what others have said, give them the chance to refine or change what they have said, and give you time to decide what to ask next especially when you have been surprised by what they have said;
3. *Not asking open ended questions*, e.g. beginning with "What" or "How". Open ended questions are important to enable you to find out what is really going on. Thinking about how you will phrase your questions before you meet others is a good thing to do, especially in situations where you might only get to ask them one question;
4. *Not continuing to Ma-Ma repeatedly* and, therefore, not being able to lead the conversation to uncover what you really need to know.

Every sales book you read will push the idea of asking questions. Instead just "bring Ma-Ma to the table".

DIALOGUE – THE "MA-MA" TECHNIQUE

M Mirror or reflect the other party's words/emotions, "So (reflect back words)?" For example, So the boss hurt himself on the golf course yesterday? YES

- Shows the other party you are listening and validating their feelings.
- Confirms what you have heard.
- Gets a yes from the other party.
- Gives you time to figure out what to ask about next.

A Ask a question exploring common ground or expressed need, "What … ?" "How … ?".

For example, How much do people know about the situation?

- Uncovers other party's hidden needs.
- Builds the common ground between you.
- Opens a way ahead allowing you to generate issues and options.
- Gives you needed information to construct a solution or way forward.

Business Development Tip: Bring Ma-Ma to the Table

DIALOGUE – FIND A RELATIONSHIP THREAD TO FOLLOW UP

Relationship threads represent the things we know about each other (and sometimes share), which bind us together. The list below provides the examples needed to understand what I am talking about. Essential relationship threads are the people, things, and experiences we love and which, when shared with others, provide the basis for our relationships. The more threads, the stronger the relationship. You might have relationship threads in common with strangers, but because you are unaware they exist, you are strangers to each other. Close friends and family have many relationship threads in common but over time, especially when not supplemented with new common experiences, these relationship threads can be brittle and even break. Meanwhile new people enter our lives all the time and some become even closer family and friends than those of years before.

One of the goals of this book is to remind you that *sales begin with relationships, relationships begin with dialogue, and dialogue begins with questions.* Bring Ma-Ma to the table and ask questions to uncover the relationship threads of the person you are talking to. You don't have to have relationships in common with someone to like or admire them, but you do need to know what the threads are if you want to stay in touch. The more relationship threads you have in common, the easier it will be for your lives to intertwine should you wish that to happen.

There are five things you need to know about relationship threads:

1. Everyone has relationship threads.
2. Relationship threads evolve over time.

3. You need to ask questions to uncover other people's relationship threads.

4. Relationship threads lead you to their iceberg of interests.

5. Relationship threads provide non-sales opportunities to stay in touch.

DIALOGUE – EVERYONE HAS RELATIONSHIP THREADS

I was setting up for a workshop to facilitate the merger of Exxon and Mobil when an oil executive approached me to say he was 100% against the integration efforts. "You are just running these workshops to figure out who you want to fire. With two people for every one job, it is obvious half the people in this room today will be losing their job". It was a bad start to what was going to be a tough day. Although no one was going to lose their jobs and the workshop was designed to help attendees fit into the new organisational structure, it was clear everyone was anxious and half the people were as upset as the gentleman selected to speak to me. Realising I had to deal with this before starting, or else I risked a failed workshop, I used the Ma-Ma technique, acknowledged his upset, and asked him what he planned to do. "I'm taking the package and retiring early", he said. "Wow that's a big change and one that requires a lot of planning. Why don't you focus on that as your change in today's workshop and not worry about your future with the company", I ventured. The man stayed for the day and at the end of the workshop he stuck around to thank me for suggesting he use the day to plan his retirement. He said, "It was the best day I've spent in years". Simply by using the Ma-Ma technique, validating his emotion, and asking a question to identify a relationship thread, I could sell the idea that he stay in the workshop. When others saw he was staying, they stayed too, and the day was a success. I'm sure if I could find him again today, he'd remember that fateful day which kicked off the start of his retirement.

Everyone has things they love to talk about, to spend their time on, to dream about. Everyone in the world has passions that bring light to their eyes and excitement to their voice. It is almost certain these things won't match what you want to sell them, but if you put their interests ahead of your own, if you focus on and help develop their relationship threads, it will be like threading wire between two towers. Just like when the engineers built Hong Kong's Tsing Ma bridge, as you add more threads they can support a bridge and, with time, the bridge between the two of you will be able to carry cars and trains and withstand the storms of time.

Business Development Tip: Use Ma-Ma to Find Relationship Threads

DIALOGUE – RELATIONSHIP THREADS EVOLVE OVER TIME

I went to my dentist a few years ago, after a long interval, and he asked me about my two kids and my accounting career. By that time, I had three kids and worked as a negotiation consultant. Since my dentist only updated his record of my relationship threads when I visited for a treatment (not often enough he tells me), his attempt at dialogue was a bit out of date. People's interests change, relationship threads evolve over time. You need to stay in touch if you want to keep your conversations current. If you are an account manager, you realise there is a limit to how many relationships you can reasonably stay up to date with. One of my wealth management clients had so many relationships to look after he could not even spend a few hours a year with each client. When I asked him how many clients he had which he could identify relationship threads for, he only pointed to the 20% which were most important to him in terms of business referrals, etc. I wasn't surprised. He had too many supposed relationships to be responsible for. I laugh when HSBC email me every few years introducing their next relationship manager. They never ask to meet me and demonstrate no interest in me. Their attempt at digital sales fails my test of relationship threads. They are so bad, they even mail me flyers written only in Chinese even though my account clearly states my preference for English correspondence. If you want to sell effectively, you need to know and follow relationship threads and do your best to keep these up to date over time.

DIALOGUE – YOU NEED TO ASK QUESTIONS TO UNCOVER OTHER PEOPLE'S RELATIONSHIP THREADS

My wife, a kindergarten teacher, used to hate social functions where she didn't know anyone. She noticed how people would stop asking her questions when they learnt she was a teacher. In her head (then), people at cocktail parties in Hong Kong only wanted to talk to lawyers, accountants, and investment bankers. Once my wife learnt the Ma-Ma technique, she became an expert in social functions and asked others all about their lives, finding herself deep in conversation with strangers in no time. Now my wife notes how many people she meets that actually ask about her life and she realises very few do, but those who do make her feel they are more interesting to follow up and meet again. Most people are actually shy with strangers and untrained at asking questions, so conversation remains very superficial. It needn't be this way. Bring Ma-Ma to the table and you will soon be learning lots of things about other people. If they in turn ask about you, it is a bonus, but just like when they string the first wire to build a suspension bridge, the first questions need to come from one side and it might as well be you. As they say, the best conversationalist at the party is the one people know the least about because they are always asking questions of other people.

Business Development Tip: Keep Renewing Your Relationship Threads

DIALOGUE – RELATIONSHIP THREADS LEAD YOU TO THEIR ICEBERG OF INTERESTS

Perhaps one of the most important things you need to learn about selling yourself, your ideas, or your professional services, is that *it isn't about selling at all. It is about following relationship threads to uncover other people's interests and then figuring out how your ideas or services fit their interests.* Don't think you can start talking to people about your passion and think they will be interested. Some might be interested, but most won't, and you'll be wasting your precious time. Instead, focus on their interests and then find a way to achieve your goals by fulfilling theirs.

People, like organisations, have both stated and unstated needs and wants, which can be further subdivided into either emotional or rationale needs and wants. Like an iceberg which shows a bit of itself above the water but has more of its mass hidden below the water line, people too expose a small part of their character in public, so time and questions are needed to fully uncover another person's needs and wants. The following table will give you an idea of what awaits you when you bring Ma-Ma to the table and follow relationship threads to better get to know others.

DIALOGUE – ICEBERG OF NEEDS AND WANTS

	Emotional	Rationale
Stated	Have fun.	Buy guitar lessons.
Unstated	Live music venues are more fun than staying at home.	Deeply moved by blues guitar sounds.

Business Development Tip: Follow Relationship Threads to Undercover Needs and Wants

DIALOGUE – RELATIONSHIP THREADS PROVIDE NON-SALES OPPORTUNITIES TO STAY IN TOUCH

Continuing the previous example, if your target client loves live music and blues guitar you can stay in touch with him by inviting him to a blues guitar show or forwarding a social media post about a favourite blues guitarist. I call this *following relationship threads for non-sales opportunities to stay in touch*. The recipient will almost always take interest in what you have sent because it matches their needs or wants. This opens the door for an opportunity to spend time together and these unplanned non-business times together are when you tend to learn the most about opportunities for business. This is targeted time together and is a lot more diverse than simply going for drinks after work (not something I recommend for business development).

Below is a list of the most common relationship threads. The list is finite and all you need to do is ask questions to find out what your target person is passionate about. Everyone is passionate about something.

Relationship Threads

Work
- Work life
- The company
- Professions
- Organisation development

Personal and relationship
- Parenting
- Marriage
- Family
- Grandparenting
- Kids
- In-laws
- Celebrations and anniversaries
- Investing
- Property
- Food/Diet
- Homemaking
- People/gossip
- Relationships
- Future
- Health
- Career development

Subject knowledge
- History
- Economics
- Science
- IT
- Education, learning, knowledge

Community and social issues
- Environments
- Current events
- Religion/spirituality
- Community groups (scouts)
- Charities
- Policies, procedures, and regulations
- Poverty
- Bureaucracy
- Globalisation
- Politics (local, provincial, state, national, international)
- Death and dying
- Ethics/corruption

Hobbies
- Food
- Pets, pet care
- Pet training
- Cinema
- Theatre
- Museums
- Reading/writing
- Nature
- Theme parks
- Spectators (sports)
- Participation sports
- Collecting (stamps, maps, coins, cars, antiques, books)
- Shopping
- Travel

Business Development Tip: Use Relationship Threads as Non-Sales Opportunities to Stay in Touch

RECORD/SYNCH – BULLDOG OPPORTUNITY TRACKER

When I was a boy, my family had a British Bulldog named Butch. Bulldogs are famous for their large heads, wrinkled face, and very strong jaw, complete with jutting teeth and slobbering jowls. Butch loved to grab things in his teeth and let us try to pull it away from him. Butch would always win. Being three boys meant we weren't always the best behaved with our dog. We'd feed him toads, friends' shoes, and we even tried tabasco sauce to see the resulting waterfall of slobber that would erupt from his mouth. The most fun was taking an old bicycle tyre and playing tug of war. Realising Butch would not loosen his grip of the bicycle tyre, we became adventurous and began lifting the tyre high enough off the ground to see if he would let go once in the air. Realising going airborne wasn't enough to get our dog to let go of the bicycle tyre we then began lifting him in the air and swinging the bicycle tyre around our heads, six feet off the ground. Possibly in panic or simply through dogged determination, Butch would never let go of the tyre.

Hence the name Bulldog Opportunity Tacker. Once you step up the quantity and quality of your business development dialogues, you will begin surfacing a lot of opportunities. It is important to capture these opportunities as soon as they arise and before you forget them. Opportunities include leads for business, suppliers, referrals, friendships, information, etc. The Bulldog Opportunity Tracker is essential for successful business development for several reasons, but first and foremost, like Butch holding onto the bicycle tyre, good business development professionals never let go. I have pursued some opportunities for ten years before finally winning the business. Likewise, I have let go and lost out to competitors, only to find out later that I lost out because I stopped pursuing the client in question.

When using the Bulldog Opportunity Tracker, you only need to capture the essential details of the opportunities you surface so that you can refer to your list and follow up. You can capture your key pieces of information either digitally or on paper, but whichever format you choose, the list must be visible to ensure follow-up. My recommended format is paper based, on your desk or in your diary. I include the Bulldog Opportunity Tracker in the Appendix. It includes spaces to capture the following important pieces of information:

- *Date* – so you can refer specifically to when you found it, where to find it in the many in-trays now bombarding our lives.
- *Target Organisation* – so you remember which company you are dealing with.

- *Target Contact* – this is the name of the person with whom you must follow up.
- *Opportunity* – describe your opportunity in just a few words so you can remember.
- *Referrer* – this is the person who has referred you, an essential piece of information to ensure you say thank you.
- *Source* – this is where you note how the opportunity arose to facilitate finding the thread and following up, for example, face to face, telephone, conference call, Skype, email, LinkedIn, Messenger, WhatsApp, Facebook, WeChat, newspaper, cocktail party, chamber of commerce, public workshop, client work, etc.

Business Development Tip: Capture All Opportunities before You Forget

RECORD/SYNCH – SALES OVERSIGHT USING THE BULLDOG OPPORTUNITY TRACKER

The Bulldog Opportunity Tracker is a *very* effective tool for reviewing your sales efforts or those of your team to see where they are falling short and what they might do to improve. Here is a list of the most common problems surfaced by using the Bulldog Opportunity Tracker:

1. *Very few entries* – this suggests the user is either not meeting the right people, not meeting enough people, not recording opportunities which arise, not recognising opportunities when they arise, or not asking the right questions. Comparing the Bulldog Opportunity Tracker with the user's meeting schedule will quickly identify if the shortage of entries results from who they are or aren't meeting, or from the dialogues they are having.
2. *Date* – this will give you an idea of how many opportunities are being surfaced in a given time period.
3. *Organisation* – this will give you a quick idea who the user is meeting with or talking about.
4. *Contact* – this will tell you if the user is meeting the right people (i.e. people with money and authority to approve the purchase) and following up referrals.

5. *Opportunity* – this will tell you what sort of leads are being generated and whether the user is having the right discussions.
6. *Referrer* – this is useful to see where your business is coming from, so you can say thank you and maximise your attention to these key individuals.
7. *Source* – since social media is also important for referrals, pay attention to the medium of where your leads are coming from, so you can optimise your attention to these sources (e.g. golf club) and minimise your time spent trying to do business development in places where few, if any, leads arise (e.g. Facebook).

Business Development Tip: Use the Bulldog Opportunity Tracker to Identify Weaknesses in Your Sales Process

RECORD/SYNCH – UPDATE YOUR ADDRESS BOOK, CRM, OR CONTACT DATABASE

You are in a taxi on the way back to your office and you are looking at the dozen business cards you have just collected at an evening gathering for the alumni of your university. You realise there are a few people for whom you didn't collect any business cards, so their contact details are hard to get, but for those cards you did collect, what do you do with them? Most people either throw the cards away or put them into piles by source, date, or name. Good business development professionals have a way of capturing the data for future use and follow-up (Figure 2.7). Here is what I have found to be the minimum required action to ensure follow-up:

1. Bring business cards to exchange with others. It is hard to collect business contacts if you have no cards yourself to prompt the exchange. In some cultures, like Hong Kong, the business card exchange is like a dance of courtship. In other cultures, like Canada, very few people carry business cards and even fewer exchange them. It is good practice and greatly facilitates follow-up, so I recommend that you carry cards and exchange whenever you feel it will be useful to do so.

FIGURE 2.7
Biz Card Coding.

2. As soon as you get a moment, code the cards which you have received noting the following essential bits of information:
   a. How this person relates to you, e.g. C=client, S=supplier, F=family or friend, P=participant, N=network or colleague, etc.
   b. Date you met.
   c. Where you met.
   d. Relationship threads, if any.
   e. Motivational dialect, if apparent.
   f. Anything you have promised to do in follow-up to your meeting
3. Give the cards to your secretary or assistant for him/her to input into your address book, CRM software, or contact database, whichever is applicable.

Business Development Tip: Keep Your Address Book Current

RECORD/SYNCHRONISE – QUALIFY YOUR LEAD OR OPPORTUNITY

Not all leads are equal and you only have a limited number of hours in your day. Correctly qualifying leads and prioritising your sales efforts is one of the easiest ways to differentiate experienced and inexperienced salespeople. When I was just starting out in sales and my partner tried telling me something about the difference between suspects and prospects, I was unable to differentiate the two and would chase every opportunity which arose. As you gain experience, you become much more adept at chasing the best opportunities. Young dogs seem to be forever chasing squirrels up trees without ever catching one. Old dogs know not to waste their energy chasing squirrels up trees because they know their chance of catching one is extremely limited. There are four things you should consider when qualifying your leads appearing in your Bulldog Opportunity Tracker. These include:

- *The value to you* – if it is a very valuable opportunity, like when I was asked to pursue an opportunity to help the owner of Uber, you should give it higher marks than, say, helping a charity, which will not pay or give you much profile.
- *The value to them* – if your help, ideas, or service can bring great value to your prospective client then this is much more interesting than chasing an opportunity where they don't really need you.
- *Competitiveness* – every buyer has a choice and even if you are the only vendor, they still have the choice to do it themselves, do nothing, or hire you. Another sign of an experienced salesperson is that they know ALL about the competition. Charities know how much prospective donors are giving to competing charities. Suppliers know which other professionals their prospective clients are working with. Leaders know which other leaders' ideas people are following. You need to know your competition and conservatively assess your chance of beating them.
- *Relationship* – you need to honestly assess how well you know the target person identified in your Bulldog Opportunity Tracker. If you don't know them or any of their relationship threads, there is little chance you will successfully sell to them.

When you are just starting out, it is useful to measure each of the above criteria out of five. When I was introduced to consult the owner of Uber, I had to explain why I wasn't optimistic to win the business. For various reasons, the owner of Uber had gone public saying he was seeking help from a leadership and negotiation consultant. There are a finite number of us in the world, but I was doubtful of winning the business. Despite this, the person referring me insisted I pursue the opportunity, so I did and I never heard back from Uber. I was not surprised. Here is how I assessed this opportunity:

- Value to me = 5 (this engagement would have brought significant acclaim if successful).

- Value to Uber = 3 (I didn't think I was offering a lot more than they could get from leading international consultants based in the USA).
- Competitiveness = 5 (since Uber faced most of its problems in Asia and since I had considerable experience in Asia, we felt I could win).
- Relationship = 0 (even the person referring me didn't know the target personally, and for this reason, I felt little chance of winning).
- Total = 13.

Qualifying leads only becomes important when you have competing choices for the use of your time. When I was starting out and had no clients, pursuing Uber by flying to San Francisco and trying to open doors with a free lecture might have made sense, but after years of client work, I was lucky enough to have other opportunities to pursue which qualified higher, for example, general insurance client (15 points), government client (16 points), hotel client (17 points), family time (18 points), etc. Qualifying leads doesn't mean you don't eventually pursue everything, it simply allows you to chase the things you will likely win first and leave the squirrels in the tree for later.

Before leaving this topic, some might wonder why family time appears on my list of qualified leads. In deciding how to invest my summer holidays, I needed to compare assured work in Sri Lanka with annual summer leave with family. Despite really wanting to help my client in Sri Lanka, I had to decline the opportunity and fly to Canada instead. I didn't need to sit down and rate these two opportunities because once you become an experienced sales professional, qualifying leads becomes second nature. Below is what it would have looked like if I had qualified the opportunities. I took the holiday and am now actively pursuing alternate dates to visit Sri Lanka.

Comparing Opportunities

	Helping Uber Founder	Speaking in Sri Lanka	Family Holiday
Value to me	5	5	5
Value to them	3	3 (other speakers available)	5
Competitiveness	5	4 (they told me I was their second choice and #1 wasn't available)	4 (there are other opportunities to be together)
Relationship	0	4 (it would be hurt by saying no)	4 (80th birthday parties only come once in a lifetime)
Total	13	16	18

Business Development Tip: Prioritise Your Opportunities

ACT – DECIDE WHAT TO DO NEXT

Once you have made your plan, engaged in dialogue, and recorded your findings, you must act. It might sound crazy, but a lot of inexperienced salespeople stop at this point for fear of being rejected. Rejection is part of the game of sales. You will never achieve a 100% hit rate (% of opportunity won). What you want to achieve is a high hit rate on what you have qualified as being valuable to pursue. What is a good percentage? Some say the average hit rate is 25%. My hit rate is over three times higher because I do a much better job qualifying leads early in the process. Do I rule out opportunities I might have won if I had pursued them sooner? It is possible, but since I continue dialogue with my clients, I don't think so.

We were a bunch of friends sitting around the outdoor tables at Singapore's famous East Coast seafood restaurants. I was relatively new into sales and I realised I was eating with a bunch of seasoned service professionals with considerable sales experience. I asked them, "What do you do when you pursue an opportunity but the client eventually sales no?" "I go home and cry", said the first person. It is natural to feel defeated in such situations. You become much more resilient when you are in sales. "I get angry and throw things at the wall in my office", said the next one, frustrated that he invested his time in a losing proposition when he could have better invested his time anywhere else, even sleeping. "I turn off my phone and study the situation to diagnose what went wrong so I can ensure it never happens again", said the third consultant. Everyone thought that was a good idea. Apart from me there remained one more person to respond. Scott, a former professional footballer from Scotland, who became famous as a leading trainer for Dale Carnegie in Asia, sat quietly listening. "Scott, how about you?" someone asked. "I call up the client and tell them it's not a problem they have chosen to work with someone else this time. I tell them it's normal not to give all their work to one consultant. I tell them I'm okay with their decision and ask who they have chosen and why. I usually find out the answer and later I call them back and find out how the other consultant performed, to understand their strengths and weaknesses, and better understand the needs and wants of my client". Upon hearing Scott's answer, all of us were stunned because we also knew Scott had the strongest client relationships of anyone at the table that evening. It was a masterclass in losing well.

I'll return to the topic of clients that say no, but at this stage, to optimise your revenue and use of your time, it is important to translate your qualified leads into action. There are three things you should do with the leads on your Bulldog Opportunity Tracker.

1. *Pursue personally* – If it is a strong lead, in your area of expertise, and you are available to lead the work if you win it, then you should pursue the opportunity personally. Clients always prefer when the sales efforts are made by the service professional that will be doing the work. It allows the client to begin feeling comfortable with you before choosing to work with you. Likewise, if you don't win this choice piece of work, you will have personal knowledge of why you lost out to the competition, and you'll know what to change for next time.

2. *Refer to others* – It is impossible to be an expert in any given area and accept every opportunity that comes your way. If the opportunity isn't in your area of expertise, you should certainly refer others who will do a better job. You might assist them and win referral fees but most important is that if they do a great job your client will be happy and you want your client to be happy. If you do it yourself and fail to do a great job (because it is outside your area of expertise), you risk disappointing your client and worse, you will dilute your brand by causing confusion in the market about what you do. As you grow your team of experts it will be natural that you win more business than you can fulfil. This is a great problem to have because the more people you have working for you, the more money you will be making (but you'll be managing others rather than practising your expertise).

3. *Note for later* – There are many reasons you might simply want to keep note of opportunities for later. The situation might be evolving. The client might be waiting for budget approval. The client might want your service but not yet have a need. You might have better qualified leads to pursue first. It is valuable to keep track of the lead, even if you only note it for later because it will give you the chance to follow up with your client and dialogue on the evolving needs and wants regarding this opportunity.

Business Development Tip: Do Something with Every Opportunity

ACT – RESEARCH

As soon as I was referred the opportunity of work with a leading European pharmaceutical company to help them influence government policy in Asia, I knew I had to get busy doing research. The terms used in the initial briefing were unknown to me, and the scientists were so unused to talking to non-scientists, they found it hard to explain complex scientific terms in simple ways. My research was invaluable to refining my proposal and eventually winning the business. In the span of a week, I went from knowing nothing at all about what they were talking about to sounding at least a little knowledgeable about their topic. There are some very important things you should research BEFORE writing your proposal. These include:

- *Subject* – As explained above, you need to know what the client is talking about, otherwise you risk losing out to a competitor who has a better grasp of the industry, the product, the company, the situation. Nothing can replace doing your homework. As the Boy Scout motto reminds us, *Be prepared.*
- *People* – Do all you can to identify the key stakeholders and all you can to find out about them as early as possible. Who will be approving the budget, who will be reviewing the proposal, who is your target audience, etc. You don't want any surprises once you get started working and the better you uncover the personalities beforehand, the better you can adjust what you say and how to say it (see motivational dialects and value propositions).
- *Needs versus wants* – The client will probably tell you what they want but they don't always know what they need. Think of when you go to your doctor. You want to get rid of your headache. You later find out that you need to stop eating cheese because the doctor has discovered you to be lactose intolerant. Experts can diagnose the difference between needs and wants but most people can't. It gets tricky sometimes because the client might insist on buying the service they want, e.g. a head massage, when in fact

what they need is to change their diet. Your experience helps a lot in these situations, but even experienced service professionals will be confronted with new situations throughout their career. Do your homework and test your assumptions to be sure you are correct, e.g. maybe their headaches are caused by dehydration and not lactose intolerance.

- *Competition* – As mentioned earlier, you can't win 100% of the opportunities that come your way. Some opportunities arise because clients are forced to seek three offers before choosing one. I was asked once by a good client of mine to respond to a request for proposal but she said I wouldn't win the work because they wanted another supplier. She simply needed three quotes so they could satisfy policy and hire my competitor. I didn't appreciate her wanting to waste my time, but since she was a good client, I obliged by sending a quick off-the-shelf proposal, which I didn't win. Apart from helping you manage your time, doing research on your competitors should also inform your pricing and your service offering. I am considered relatively expensive compared to the average in my market. I work in English or French and I serve clients globally. When competing with local consultants offering services in Cantonese in Hong Kong, I know the market price is lower and people prefer services rendered in their first language. Experienced salespeople know the competition and their market position and propose accordingly. If you don't know the competition in your market, start doing your homework. Check advertisements, go to their public workshops, ask people in your network, and meet them. Get informed.

- *Budget* – Separate from knowing competitor pricing, you also need to know your client's budget. "What's your budget?" is a common question heard in proposal meetings. If you are asked this question, you typically react in two ways. Firstly, you are a bit offended, thinking this to be confidential, and second, you will usually quote a figure lower than your actual budget, hoping to get a deal and look better to your boss. Knowing the budget isn't just about the total forecast spend, it is also about where the money will come from (sometimes projects are financed out of different budgets), what the money will be used for (sometimes there is budget available for things outside what you are discussing), and how the budget will play out over the life of the project which sometimes lasts several years.

- *History* – I often find myself called to assist clients that have previously hired less experienced consultants thinking they were saving money, but later found out they wasted all their money because the consultant was a disaster. Know the client's experience with previous consultants, the history of the situation they are trying to resolve, who caused the problem if there is one, and what they have done so far to resolve the situation, if anything. A good way to get answers is to ask your client, "Who else can I speak with to gather further information prior to writing my proposal?"

ACT – CONTINUE DIALOGUE

Sometimes months or even years go by before you action an opportunity. It is important to continue dialogue with your prospective client throughout the intervening period to assess how the opportunity is evolving and what else is arising, if anything. Some opportunities will fade away or get fulfilled by others. Some opportunities suddenly become priority and proposals are required faster than you thought. Sometimes new opportunities arise. It is always good to remember that in the business of sales, the solution is in the dialogue.

Business Development Tip: Find Out What You Don't Know

ACT – WRITE AND PRESENT PROPOSAL

There are lots of books telling you how to write and present your proposal. I don't need to go into details here, other than to share what I consider to be the most important elements at this step of the process. The first thing the client wants to see is price and normally, the last thing consultants like to show is price. I have learnt from my work in negotiation that the longer you make the client wait to know the pricing the more displeased they will be. When I present pricing, I like to give clients more detail rather than less so that clients can figure out how to save money. You know they want to do this so make it easy for them to figure this out. I also like to itemise everything in the proposal (e.g. fees, discounts, materials, expenses). I also attach my standard fee schedule and terms so that clients get the full picture. I don't discuss price first but I don't make it hard to find either. My proposals normally include the following elements:

- *Brief* – Using the client's words, I start with a paragraph describing what the clients wants me to do and why.
- *Outline* – Next is my response to their brief. Sometimes, this breaks into various parts, for example research, pre-work, delivery, follow-up. As often as possible, I make this outline as actual as possible, including timing to the minute, and I normally use this outline to direct my work as speaker or trainer.
- *Logistics* – This section includes everything that needs to be done before my intervention such as printing of materials and room set-up. I attach generic details so this section isn't long, but it needs to be clear what you expect the client to do and what you will do.
- *Investment* – This is where I discuss fees, discounts, materials, expenses.
    - My fees are based on the commoditised rates for someone of my calibre of experience.
    - Discounts (and premiums) enable me to tailor the fees from my standard fee schedule into the local market or situation experienced by the client. I give discounts for repeat business, referrals, convenient timing and location, not-for-profits, needy countries, etc.
    - Material costs – these vary considerably client to client, due to the nature of tools required for their situation. I don't aim to make money on materials, just enough to cover the carrying costs, which in Hong Kong can be quite high.
    - Expenses – I also don't aim to make any profit on my expenses, but likewise, I don't like losing money either. My proposals include best estimates of expenses to be incurred and my terms suggest that if expenses are to vary beyond what it estimated, then they are subject to agreement. Clients don't like getting ripped off on expenses, so I offer receipts for everything.
- *Next Steps* – All my proposals finish with a section where I remind the client what they and I need to do next.
- *Appendices* – These normally include my bio, client list, standard fee schedule, pre-work (if any), venue preparation checklist, etc.

- *Links* – I attach links to all my social media, websites, APP, and TED talk, YouTube, etc.
- *Contact details* – I always ensure they know how to reach me and I invite clients to discuss with their colleagues and call me to refine the proposal. I mark all my proposals DRAFT but seldom find myself needing to change them.

My goal writing a proposal is to leave the client with as accurate a projection as possible regarding what I will do, when, and how much it will cost. When time is tight, I include a deposit invoice to lock in my dates, order materials, and book flights as required. In writing my proposals, I aim to leave clients saying, "Peter is an outstanding resource and quite easy to work with". My proposals aren't perfect. Ideally, proposals should include graphics, multi-media content, etc. Also, in a perfect world, you should present your proposal rather than simply email it to clients. You want to observe and manage their reaction to your proposal, but when you email your proposal to the client, you can't manage their reaction. The best you can do is to follow up by calling and asking if they received it and whether they have any questions. In my experience, the lower the person you are dealing with is in the organisation chart, the more questions they will have about your proposal. If you are dealing this low on the totem pole, you may question the relationship score you gave when qualifying the lead in question.

> **Business Development Tip:** Keep Close to Your Proposal and Your Prospect's Reaction

ACT – NEGOTIATE SCOPE AND PRICING

Here is not the place to repeat what I have written in my book on *Negotiation: Mastering Business in Asia*. There are many things you need to know to be ultimately successful, but these three will make a big difference for you when negotiating.

1. Most clients want to squeeze a deal out of your proposal. Don't consider this behaviour to be devaluing your offer, they simply feel the need to negotiate. The need to negotiate can be factual (e.g. budget is too small) or cultural (Chinese love to negotiate, the English not so much).

2. Start high, knowing they want to negotiate down and be sure to remain in dialogue with the client, because if you are too high, they will talk to your competitor first and cut you out of the deal. The best is to quote high but remain in dialogue.

3. Remember, everything is negotiable, not just fees. For example, scope is negotiable, quality is negotiable, timing is negotiable.

My book on negotiation provides a lot of tips for service selling. I encourage you to download it (or order it from Amazon) and read it. Any questions, just let me know. I answer readers' questions all the time.

Business Development Tip: Be a Star Negotiator

ACT – DELIVER QUALITY SERVICE

Obviously, good service leaves the client happy and a happy client leads to more work, referrals, and positive testimonials. Unhappy clients are the opposite. One thing people often overlook is the opportunity to dialogue on other needs and wants the client may have while you are busy delivering the current engagement. Training your service delivery team in the skills of dialogue selling will generate more leads and fill your Bulldog Opportunity Tracker.

Business Development Tip: Train Your Service Delivery Team in Dialogue Selling

Before leaving the topic of quality service delivery, it is sobering to realise that problems still occur, even in the best planned situations. A good thing to remember is that clients don't hold you to 100% perfection since they know this would be unreasonable. What clients do expect of you, however, is rapid and effective service recovery after mistakes take place. This doesn't always mean you can replace something like a bad meal. When I was involved debriefing the MH17 airline disaster, where hundreds died after their aircraft was hit by a missile while flying over a war zone, there was no way the client could replace the lost souls. Service recovery in this instance related to how well they kept the families of the victims and other travellers informed about what was going on. This particular airline has not financially recovered from this accident (and another missing plane was lost in the same year), but their service has resumed and the families of the victims have been compensated.

> **Business Development Tip:** You Are Only as Good as Your Last Engagement

ACT – REQUEST AND RESPOND TO FEEDBACK

Another surprisingly uncommon step in the sales process is to request and respond to feedback. I'm not talking about email-based service assessments like you receive after checking out from your favourite hotel. I'm talking about asking for a time to meet face to face and dialogue the good, the bad, and the ugly, regarding the service you and your team have just provided. The sooner you debrief service delivery, the better. I like to do this right away, but fewer and fewer clients seem willing to do so, as preference for autonomous feedback using apps like Survey Monkey is replacing the traditional client debriefing.

Apart from learning obvious things about the engagement you have just completed for a client, feedback sessions also provide non-sales opportunities to follow up where you can learn about other opportunities following on from your present engagement. I recommend you request a debriefing every time you provide service.

It isn't enough to request and receive client feedback. If they give you feedback, they will be expecting that you do something with it. When I give feedback in a restaurant, I expect, the next time I visit, that the issue will be positively resolved and if not, I will notice and be disappointed that I wasted my time providing feedback. Instead, I recommend you not only respond to the feedback provided, but you also thank them for their feedback and tell them what you are doing with their feedback. If you are not doing anything, you should still thank them and explain why no action will be undertaken. You want clients to talk to you and thanking them for their feedback is a great way to keep them talking. The more your clients talk with you, the less they talk with your competitors.

> **Business Development Tip:** Continuous Improvement is the Sign of a Great Professional

ACT – COLLECT FEES AND EXPENSES

I've never read a book on sales that talked about billing and accounts receivable as part of the sales process, but from my experience doing procurement negotiations, I realise this is very much part of the sales process because it is often the last thing the client remembers of your work, and you need this to be a positive experience while collecting 100% of your fees and expenses. What have I learnt over the years that you should know? My experience here includes the ten years I spent working for one of the largest firms in the world. Clients hate surprises. In a perfect world, your invoice and expenses should match your proposal. Problems arise when there is scope creep (the situation forces more work than forecast) or unforeseen expenses. All variations should be negotiated and agreed BEFORE you send your invoice, otherwise you are pretty well assured to have a collection problem.

If you haven't kept track of time and expenses prior to the billing stage, I suggest you take a conscious decision whether you want to "invest" the unbillable time into maintaining a better client relationship or risk damaging the client relationship (sometimes irreplaceably) by surprising them with unforeseen fee increases. Put yourself in the buyer's shoes. You wouldn't like it either.

If you decide you want to collect what you feel is your due, then the best approach is to engage in dialogue about the reasons for and quantum of the variation in fees and expenses and then negotiate a reasonable outcome. I suggest you go in expecting nothing while aiming for 100% recovery. Ensure you maintain your best decorum and friendly approach while persistently insisting on full payment. You might be able to say non-payment will result in the cut-off of services, but unless you have a monopoly, the buyer is unlikely to care that you appear threatening or upset. There is pretty much always another supplier. Collection problems might flag poor due diligence of your clients before commencing work. One of the important aspects to consider when assessing the client value to you is whether they will pay. I have walked away from chronic non-payers.

The collection process is also a useful non-sales opportunity to stay in touch with your client. Use the opportunity to discuss the client's needs and wants and you might just find that in addition to collecting your fees and expenses, you also win more work.

Before leaving this topic, it is useful to remind you of the importance of keeping timesheets for everything you do. Most readers will hate this idea. Few will have experience doing so and those who do (e.g. people in big firms) typically hate it. The reason I do so is because there is nothing more valuable than your time record and that of your team members when assessing how long it has taken for you to complete an engagement and how long it might take you next time. A common problem for people new to services selling is predicting how many hours or days an engagement will take to complete and all the expenses incurred along the way. The more experienced you are, and the more you study the time and expenses of similar jobs (or the same job last year), the more accurate your proposal will be and the easier your collection process.

The big firms record time in six-minute units. In my small firm, I'm happy recording two, four, six, or eight hours per day, based on an 8-hour day. I also record and bill for overtime. I aim to collect 100% of my time and expenses. I have very few collection problems. I manage fee issues up front in the proposal negotiation, by negotiating my discount. I don't let my clients play around with my standard rates or expense projections. I give clients plenty of opportunity to minimise expenses by giving me assistants, printing in-house, using their facilities, using their corporate rates, etc. I maintain control of travel arrangements since this is my time, but I do factor in my travel time when calculating fees. I once travelled 36 hours for a 16-hour engagement.

Business Development Tip: Keep Track of Your Time

PLAN – UPDATE RELATIONSHIP DATABASE/CRM/ ADDRESS BOOK AND SET CONTACT FREQUENCY

There are several things to follow up after an engagement and one of the things that often gets overlooked is to update the contact details for your client. While you carry out your work, you will inevitably learn important details about the personalities involved. Your relationship database should include details like relationship threads, motivational dialect, organisation charts, and engagement issues to remember for next time, as well as current email and mobile phone numbers for everyone involved. You need current contact details to stay in touch. You can also note their preferred communication channels (social media, email, phone, face to face, lunch, club, sports, etc.) It is very difficult to keep your contact database up to date so, as much as possible, you should be updating this BEFORE focusing on your next engagement. Another thing you should take note of before leaving this client behind is to decide how often you should stay in touch (and how) and then programme your calendar software (or ask your staff) to remind you to stay in touch.

> **Business Development Tip:** Set Contact Frequency Based upon Needs and Importance

CONNECT – FOLLOW RELATIONSHIP THREADS FOR NON-SALES OPPORTUNITIES TO FOLLOW UP

Most service professionals I have worked with over the years hate the sales process and avoid staying in touch with their clients in between assignments. While it might be natural for non-sales professionals to dislike sales, it is VERY important for you to stay in touch with your clients. If you have decided to stay in touch quarterly, then your calendar should ping you and remind you to follow up. Add this to your "To do" list and just do it. A night out, a lunch, an email to say hello, a digital newsletter, an invitation, or a piece of information linked to one of their relationship threads, all count for non-sales opportunities to stay in touch. Everyone is busy, and your clients will forget you, but if you follow relationship threads to stay in touch, they will remember you.

In the last 20 years, every time I contacted my clients, it resulted in work or referrals from someone on my follow-up list. Most people will not respond. Some will thank you for staying in touch and a handful will fill your Bulldog Opportunity Tracker with new leads. I have also realised that failure to stay in touch results in zero leads and opportunities. The nice thing to remember is that you are not selling, you are reinforcing your relationships by following relationship threads to stay in touch, and in doing so, you are reminding your clients that you care, as well as about your value proposition, your interest in working with them again, and receiving their referrals. Do this and magic happens because people want to help each other. Do nothing and you will be assured of weakening relationships and diminishing business.

Business Development Tip: Stay in Touch

DIALOGUE – SAY THANK YOU AND ASK FOR REFERRAL

It might seem silly, but *experience shows the number one problem with service professionals is they don't fulfil their promises.* If you have got this far in the dialogue selling process then this isn't one of your problems (I hope). You have already differentiated yourself from other service providers by doing what you said.

Another way to set yourself apart from the competition is to say thank you to your clients for engaging your services. Ask for referrals or testimonials if they feel so inclined. I normally give a handwritten card to all the key people involved. This personal connection is just about all you can do nowadays while respecting the anti-corruption legislation in most jurisdictions. Considering hardly anyone says thank you and even fewer resort to old fashioned handwritten notes, you will win when you do this. I also attempt to include with my thank you card something specific about one of their relationship threads, for example, an article or book recommendation. Think about thank you notes as non-sales opportunities to stay in touch. Even if you never work for this client again, they will retain a positive view of your services if you are polite, respectful, professional, and thankful.

Business Development Tip: You're Never Too Busy to Say Thank You

RETURN TO START

If you are following my dialogue sales process flowchart, you will see that after you have done all the above steps, the flowchart brings you back to the beginning. That's natural because despite doing your best work and providing the best service possible, everything ends. Service professionals like me, that have been in the game for a generation or longer, have been repeating the process continuously the whole time. It isn't enough to just do it once and stop. If you want to be successful over the long term, you must do all these steps continuously. When you stop acting, your Bulldog Opportunity Tracker will dry up and your income will slowly end.

In my experience, *most service professionals either burn out or give up within two years of starting their business.* Failure arises for many reasons, such as insufficient expertise running a business or a weak alignment between services offered and market needs or wants. In my experience, however, the most common reason for failure is because people don't like to sell or, if they get started, they don't sustain the sales effort over the long term.

I have good news to report. *Business development and selling get easier the longer you do them.* The more experience you gain, the more your expertise is known in the market, the more referrals you will get. The more people you meet and stay in touch with, the bigger your footprint in the market becomes. Since buyers are entering and leaving the market continuously, you cannot stop creating, strengthening, and maintaining relationships, but you will find it does become easier over time. Never, never, never give up.

> **Business Development Tip:** Sales End When You Stop Selling

PLAN, CONNECT, DIALOGUE, RECORD/SYNCH, ACT

The above dialogue selling process is summarised in five steps: plan, connect, dialogue, record/synch, and follow up. If you do this continuously you will win the outcomes you want for yourself, your ideas, and your services. If you don't do this then you only have yourself to blame.

INSTILLING SALES DNA IN YOURSELF

A lot of people ask me how to instil sales behaviour in themselves. "I hate selling" is the refrain I hear all the time. I understand. I became an auditor because I didn't want to sell. Auditors don't really have to sell because companies have to have audits and all auditors have to do is get into the beauty parade, get selected, and do a great job. My auditor friends will remind me this too is selling and is not easy, but believe me, if companies didn't need to be audited there are a lot of companies that would stop buying their service. Consultants face a different reality and need to sell every time they win an engagement (international referrals are an exception fraught with their own problems).

If you really love what you do and do what you love then selling what you do isn't a burden. Once you realise you don't need to cold call like product sellers, and all you need to do is engage in dialogue to create, strengthen, and maintain relationships, you will find it a lot easier to instil the sales DNA into your behaviour. In the meantime, practice helps a lot, coaches are useful, and the most valuable motivator is banking your receipts, because there is nothing more satisfying than being paid to provide services you love to provide. Once you find your niche, it becomes a calling. If you don't feel you are there yet, don't worry, because the path is leading you in the direction you need to uncover your niche. It takes time and you need the experience, good and bad, which you gain along the way. Only then will the market consider you an expert.

Business Development Tip: It Takes Practice to Become an Effective Salesperson

INSTILLING SALES DNA INTO OTHER PEOPLE

I had a client who was very good at dialogue selling and built his business to the point he needed to hire two more people to help deliver the service. One was a commissioned salesperson who brought in the business, so the principal, and the third person could do the work they won. When the market turned down, the principal wanted to convert the third person into a sales professional. Despite coaching in the dialogue sales process, this service professional simply wasn't interested in selling and the principal was frustrated. In reviewing the options available: fire the person, force them to sell, or retain them for other reasons; we decided the best use of his talents would be to keep him 100% devoted to the professional service work and free up the principal's time instead to do more selling. Founders typically cast the broadest shadow on a market and, as a result, have the easiest time selling. By accepting that the third person wasn't the best person for selling we were simply doing what good managers should be doing all the time – figuring out how to make the most of the talent you have available.

What about getting everyone to be better at selling? I have been engaged to instil the dialogue selling process into everyone in a firm, both horizontally above a certain grade and vertically including everyone top to bottom. When everyone understands the dialogue selling process and pays attention to relationships, the result is phenomenal. When everyone uses and shares the Bulldog Opportunity Tracker, sales blossom. When everyone begins aiming to achieve five contacts a day, 25 contacts a week, 100 contacts a month, 1,200 contacts a year, sales leads skyrocket. When your social media links with your face-to-face dialogues and all your people start living the brand, your competitors will be scared. Don't worry about making sales professionals out of people who don't want to sell. Just move the whole curve forward and you will be igniting your team or organisation. It isn't magic. It is a process with five steps: plan, connect, dialogue, record, follow up.

SOME PEOPLE JUST HATE SELLING

I can't leave this topic without addressing people wanting to sell themselves for a job or promotion and people wanting to sell their ideas for change. You too might hate selling. Indeed, a lot of people apply for a job once and then stay with the same organisation for decades, preferring to stay with the same employer, even if unhappy, because they hate the idea of trying to sell themselves to another employer. A lot of people with ideas give up trying to make change happen rather than persisting with selling their ideas, because they just don't like pushing others, facing rejection, or competing for their rightful job or mind space.

If you find yourself in this group, I can't stress enough the importance of updating your concept of selling by differentiating product selling (which you probably don't like) and recognise that selling *living things (like yourself or your ideas) is really about creating and maintaining relationships and having dialogues with everyone possible*. Once you do this, you will learn what you need to convince others to hire you or follow your ideas. The solution is in the dialogue.

Business Development Tip: Some People Will Be Better than Others, but Everyone Can Sell

DNA Toolbox

The tools included in the Appendix are essential for dialogue selling professionals. If you have any questions, don't hesitate to email me. The solution is in the dialogue.

Relationship Sales Principles

You can't do sales in over 60 countries for several decades without accumulating a lot of grey hairs and wrinkles from mistakes made along the way. The next section is my gift to you in hope that you won't have to repeat my mistakes. If I had the following principles to guide my efforts when I started out, I would have probably become a lot more successful a lot earlier. I wish you success. On the other hand, you might learn best from experience (like me) and need to stumble along your path to success just like I have (and continue to do). There are plenty of problems ahead. By following my relationship sales principles, you can avoid my pitfalls in pursuit of your goals for yourself, your ideas, and your services.

3

Relationship Selling Principles

I have learnt a lot of important lessons in my life, mostly by making mistakes and then realising how to do things better the next time. I hope my experience can help you achieve your goals of selling yourself, your ideas, or your services. I set out below 21 relationship sales principles, each of which represents for me an "ah-ha" moment and an important lesson I wish I had learnt earlier. Reading this won't prevent you from having to learn other lessons, but hopefully you won't stumble on these issues and your attention can be saved for other pressing challenges facing you in your quest for success. I tell stories for each of the principles by referencing the people I learnt these principles from. I consider all these people my sales mentors and if I have been at all successful selling myself, my ideas, and my services around the world, I give all the credit to them. If you want to see farther, stand on the shoulders of giants. I thank my sales mentors for giving me the opportunity for sharing their lessons with you. Search out your own mentors. We are all on a journey and the more we can help each other along the way, the better off the journey will be for all of us.

LEARNING FROM FAMILY

It's funny I became a chartered accountant because I think I am the first accountant in the family. On my mother's side of the family, there was an abundance of doctors but my reaction to seeing blood prevented me from wanting to delve into medicine any further than playing with chemicals in the laboratory or looking at X-Rays. My father was a lumber salesman before being tapped to run the Queen

Elizabeth Hospital in Montreal because the Board realised his sales and negotiation expertise was needed for dealing with increasing government interference in the running of hospitals. The Board also realised that my father would have "skin in the game" because the hospital was founded by my mother's grandfather and it was also where her father and uncle earned their international fame as surgeon and anaesthetist respectively. The chairman of the hospital at the time was *Philip Aspinall*, a widely respected community leader and managing partner of Coopers & Lybrand in Montreal. I saw my opportunity to avoid selling and medicine. I could become an accountant and later devote my skills to hospital governance.

Life, as they say, had other plans for me. Within a few years of my qualifying as a chartered accountant, the hospital was converted into a private outpatient clinic, the Board was disbanded, and I diverted my career to being an international negotiation consultant instead. That's when I learnt the first of my relationship sales principles demonstrated by both my father (Albert) and my father-in-law (*Jean Marchand*, founder of Fondation Universitas). The principle is to *reward those who refer you or, in other words, do business with your clients*. This might be as simple as giving your clients a laminated picture of a sunset to thank them, or buying from them instead of others simply because they hired you. In following this relationship sales principle, you are further strengthening your relationship threads and making it more difficult for your competitors to muscle their way into your account. Legislation today makes it harder to reward your clients appropriately because, in places like Asia, many cultures interpreted this sales principle as kickbacks. I've had negotiation clients ask me how to deal with suppliers that offer kickbacks, saying if they work with them they will return a portion of the contract proceeds back to the buyer personally. Kickbacks are a form of corruption but saying thank you and working with your clients in an honest and transparent way is not a problem, it is good business. If your procurement policy requires three tenders for every transaction, you can still reward your clients by putting them on the tender list and giving them the chance to win the business. The time you spend together with your clients should enable them some advantage in knowing your organisation better than their competitors. Thank you Albert and Jean for reminding us to do business with our clients.

LEARNING FROM COLLEAGUES

Apart from learning sales tips from my father and father-in-law, I also learnt a lot from my negotiation and leadership development colleagues. I previously mentioned the differentiation of suspects and prospects as shared to me by Dr. David West. Suspects are people you suspect might be potential clients but you don't know until you dialogue with them. Prospects are suspects that you have met with and which, after qualifying your leads, you suspect have opportunities for you.

The colleague from whom I learnt the most about sales was *Leo Hawkins* of Melbourne, Australia. Leo had a huge network of contacts built up globally over many years of active public and private engagement. I came to know Leo as co-founder of ENS, an Australia-based negotiation consultancy with whom I became associated for several years, up until Leo's untimely passing. Leo was possibly the most intelligent man I have ever met (apart from David West and Robin Stuart-Kotze mentioned earlier). Leo and I made sales calls together in Hong Kong, Singapore, and Melbourne. In Melbourne, I introduced Leo to Colgate, a contact I had won in Hong Kong. We arrived to meet the managing director of Colgate in Leo's antique Rolls Royce. When people at Colgate Australia saw us pull into their parking lot in Leo's twelve-cylinder Rolls, they thought the chairman of Colgate USA had arrived to make a surprise visit. I learnt four things that stand out from my time with Leo:

1. *Interrupt relationship building to do your work* – After several days of sales calls with Leo, I remarked to Leo, "It appears to me that you interrupt your relationship building to do your work and as soon as your work is done you are back building relationships". "Now you are learning business development", replied Leo. It was with this intensity that Leo built his business into a highly successful international consultancy before selling his share and retiring to the coast. If you too envisage a similar level of success, you'll need to be constantly building relationships.
2. *Never cease to develop relationships* – Leo must have been raised with the value of making friends, because by the time I got to work with him towards the end of his life, it was clear he had thousands of friends and contacts stretching all the way back to his childhood.

Not only was he good at creating connections with his above average SECS Appeal (sociability, energy, curiosity, and self-confidence), his intelligence and communication skills also attracted results-oriented leaders to work with him. People who worked with Leo will remember him for all his qualities and for his passion for things like the Commonwealth War Graves Commission and for ensuring Disney finally paid royalties for using A. A. Milne's *Winnie the Pooh*.

3. *Ask for business and ask for referral* – I always found it awkward to ask my contacts for business or referrals, until I worked with Leo. Leo did this incessantly and rejoiced in successful leads, but he also used the resulting work won to go back and further reinforce the relationship with the person from whom he had won the lead. "Just do it", as Nike have made famous, and in doing so, you will realise there is nothing to be embarrassed about. Asking for help is what all successful business people do and the more you do so, the more successful you will become, enabling you to make endless referrals to others. Leo, I must add, gave more leads to others than he was given himself. People who uncover and share leads are the superhighway of the sales world and Leo was one of them. Those of you reading this book because of your interest in selling your ideas more than your services will be interested to know that Leo was just such a person, and it was his ideas that had more influence than the years he sold services.

4. *Say thank you* – Leo carried personal stationery to write thank you notes and short messages everywhere he went. He posted these constantly and, when fax arrived, he was sending thanks by fax all the time. Leo passed away prematurely but sent email thank you notes and text messages before retiring to his final resting place where he's watching to see if we remember his four-step sales process: Interrupt relationship building to do your work, never cease to develop relationships, ask for business referrals, and say thank you. Thank you Leo.

Leo's business partner and ENS co-founder *Michael Hudson* brought complementary skills to their partnership. While Leo was out front winning business, Michael Hudson was in the office figuring out how to translate Leo's leads into satisfied clients. Michael, based in Sydney and still working today, is a master trainer to all who know him. He is also a wonderful man and I miss the fun we had working together for several years. Michael taught me the importance of making everything into a system to facilitate and standardise delivery. It was in this way that ENS could train trainers and spread their best practices across the world. Whereas Michael chose to simplify and enable a wider take-up for more trainers, I preferred bespoke clients for whom I could tailor specific solutions, each engagement. Michael taught me to *ask a lot of questions to surface client's unstated needs*. Doing sales calls with Michael was always a lesson in questioning. Michael is genuinely interested in both asking and in the answers, and by uncovering the unstated and often personal needs of his prospective clients, he solidified the relationship threads which he uncovered and strengthened relationships on the go. As a detail-oriented expert, Michael takes time to record what he learns when asking questions so that he can use this information going forward. Michael was one of the earliest adopters of Apple CRM solutions, once they became available. Thank you Michael for reminding us to ask lots of questions to uncover the other party's unstated needs. "What are the needs of the other side", is the jingle Michael likes to sing in these situations.

It is normal to learn the most about a new skill when you first take it up. It isn't surprising then that my next lessons came from the consultant I spent the most time with after those already mentioned above. *Scott Lumsdaine* was a master trainer for *Dale Carnegie* when we first met. He impressed me with his storytelling and sales skills, both of which he learnt after his professional soccer career and neither of which he later confided were natural for him. Scott taught me many things and I'm sorry that distance prevents us from working together as much as we used to. The two relationship selling principles I thank Scott for teaching me are best understood together: *Some clients can't say yes but don't want to say no so it is useful to help the buyer say no if you realise they aren't going to say yes.*

Less experienced buyers, relationship-oriented people, and Asian cultures, are the three groups of people that don't want to offend others, so rather than tell you they aren't going to hire you, they instead avoid the question by not returning your calls or otherwise wasting your time. There are many reasons clients can't say yes to your proposal. It might be too expensive, they might not have authority, the budget might have been used for something else, the need might have been extinguished, they might have given the contract to your competitor, they may not like you, you might have over-qualified the lead. There are many reasons why a client doesn't want to say yes, but *every day you must choose where to invest your time and you can't afford a prospective client to be wasting your time.*

If you find yourself getting nowhere pursuing an opportunity you thought was going to work out, or a person whose mind you thought you could change but who just isn't saying yes, ask yourself if they are in that group of people that just don't want to say no.

Sometimes, you should help your buyer say no if you realise they aren't going to say yes (or help the person disagree with your idea when you realise they don't want to agree) or hire you, but not say why. Helping your contact say no to your proposal is not the type of thing you'd expect to read in a book about selling yourself, your ideas, or your services. It is counter-intuitive and that is what makes this relationship selling principle so powerful. By helping your contact overcome this distressing situation and showing them that you are okay with their decision, you are solidifying your relationship with your contact and, in so doing, you can later ask them how the engagement went with the other consultant. If you have a very good relationship, you might even be able to find out how much they paid, what they did well, where they fell short of the client's expectations etc. Ultimately, you win by creating a better relationship and gathering important market intelligence. Thank you Scott for these two important lessons.

Another colleague I greatly enjoyed working with was the Canadian *Steve Gasten*, from Vancouver. Steve lived in Hong Kong as a boy and we had some fun overlapping on the few clients I introduced to him. I learnt two important relationship selling principles from Steve, before Steve's American boss withheld money owing to me. Steve was saddened by this but couldn't do anything about it. Readers be warned. If you are in business, you will eventually meet shady people who find it easier to steal than to play by the rules. Steve worked at the time with a group of sales trainers dedicated to the telecom industry. One of their most important training points was that good salespeople *learn ALL about the competition*, so they can compete and win in as many situations as possible. You should learn about your competitor's strengths and weaknesses, their products and services, their people and prices, their clients, their strategies, etc. In the financial services business, service providers talk about share of wallet, which describes the percentage of assets managed by one financial institution. Since companies and wealthy individuals don't like to put all their eggs in one basket, they divide their assets between institutions. If, for example, the company uses JP Morgan, HSBC, and Standard Chartered Bank and split their assets roughly equally between all three institutions, then you'd say for example that Standard Chartered have 33% share of the client's wallet. By contrast, during the ten years I worked for one of the big audit firms, we never researched what our clients were doing with other firms. When I joined my then managing partner on a pitch and we found out they chose a competitor, my managing partner didn't even care to find out who it was, why we had lost, what we might do to win the business next time, etc. He was upset and didn't care about the competition. His sales development strategy consisted of merging with the competition instead.

The other relationship sales principle I learnt from Steve was to *become knowledgeable of all related prices*. Talking about price is very typical in Hong Kong, where everyone seems to know the value of everyone's house, salary, education, clothing, holidays, investments, etc. In Canada, I find the opposite to be true and, while some people share the dollar value of various assets, most people don't share, don't ask, or don't disclose even when asked. Expert sales professionals typically know more about the prices of everything than do buyers in the same market. Why? Because salespeople have to know to compete. Why don't buyers know the prices of everything if they are the buyers? Because they don't know the details from those they don't buy from. One of the most important aspects of my procurement negotiation training is to learn all about the pricing of prospective suppliers and the competition. Thank you Steve for teaching me these two important lessons.

LEARNING FROM THOUGHT LEADERS

In addition to learning from family and colleagues, I have also had the chance to learn from thought leaders alive during my lifetime. *Nelson Mandela, Ronald Reagan, Margaret Thatcher, Steve Jobs*, now all deceased, sold change in their countries through the sheer power of their ideas and persistence, and as a result, they changed the world. I have had the chance to be close to *His Holiness the Dalai Lama* several times in Dharamshala, Vancouver, and Washington, DC. He has taught, through example, the importance of compassion in the face of brutal and selfish power (PLA in Tibet). *Norman Vincent Peale* and *Robert Schuller* sold the world the power of positive thinking, an essential element of success for anyone wanting to sell themselves, their ideas, or their services in the world today. "Tough times never last, but tough people do" (Schuller). All the above leaders are examples of tough people overcoming tough times to change the world.

If you too want to change the world, you won't succeed if you don't push through the challenging times that will inevitably come your way.

Another thought leader still hard at work today is *Malcolm Gladwell*, author of *The Tipping Point: How Little Things Can Make a Big Difference* (Abacus, 2000) and other valuable books. Gladwell makes it into my list of relationship selling principles for giving me the concept of SECS Appeal. Gladwell referred to it as CESS and I simply reordered the letters to make them more memorable. To successfully sell yourself, your ideas, and your services, you need to be *S*ociable, *E*nergetic, *C*urious, and *S*elf-confident. My relationship selling principle reminds you to *keep building your SECS Appeal*. Thanks to the thought leaders mentioned for your inspiration and teaching. The world is a better place because of what you have done.

LEARNING FROM CLIENTS

I have also learnt a lot from my clients, both those that have hired me and those that haven't hired me. It is good to realise that even if you lose the proposal, you still learn and gain experience and in that way, you never lose. You will find that you learn the most once you dig in and start trying to sell yourself, your ideas, and your services, so get working.

I learnt early on that *you don't have clients, you have relationships*. Who is your most important client? If you answered with the name of a company or organisation, then you have committed the same mistake made by most people in my workshops when I ask them the same question. Once you recognise your client as the person who has hired you, and not the company they work for, then as long as they are in positions of influence, they can hire you. This is also true if they change jobs or jump companies. Stay close to these people, they are key to your success.

Mike was the managing director of a bank, whom I met through my community work. Mike asked me unexpectedly for breakfast at the Ritz Carleton and I thought I was going to get to work with his bank. At breakfast, he asked me about my experience fathering adopted children. Mike and his wife were thinking of adopting and he knew that my wife and I had adopted two children before having one of our own. Thinking I was attending a request-for-proposal breakfast, the topic of inquiry surprised me. It is uncommon for men to discuss personal topics like this without knowing each other well. He liked my work and was interested in that too, so we became friends and I helped him pro-bono by facilitating a strategy session for one of his not-for-profit organisations. Not long after our breakfast, Mike changed employers and left Hong Kong for a new bank in the Caribbean. I asked the executive director of his not-for-profit organisation for his new contact details and he said, "We threw out Mike's business card when he departed, and we don't know how to reach him". The not-for-profit was obviously disappointed he had to leave so quickly, but I persisted and tracked down Mike in Nassau. I wrote Mike, asked how he was doing and commented on the family. Mike replied immediately, saying all was well and if I knew any consultants in the Caribbean would I please make a referral. Recognising the opportunity to help my friend and visit the Caribbean at the same time, I made Mike an offer he couldn't refuse and flew to Nassau. The work went well and when Mike eventually changed employers again, I followed him again to London, the Isle of Man, and Cayman. You don't have clients, you have relationships. Create, strengthen, and maintain good relationships and opportunities will flow along these relationship threads. Thanks Mike for this valuable lesson.

Another relationship selling principle which I learnt through experience arose from training the partners of a large international law firm. They had no practice of networking internally and in their firm, as in most firms, practice experts worked in their area and had little reason or interest to dialogue with people from other departments. After training all the partners in dialogue selling, I prepared them for a live client event at a nice hotel in Shanghai's Tomorrow Square. The morning after the client event, we regrouped at the hotel for a two-hour session to debrief the client networking event, which included several hundred clients. I asked each department to meet and list all the opportunities they surfaced that evening by filling in copies of my Bulldog Opportunity Tacker. I then asked each department to share their opportunities identified by discussing one client at a time. The result was magic. Partners identified several opportunities for other departments. By networking internally to discuss these opportunities, the partners could action the opportunities uncovered. Normally, because they don't network internally, several of the opportunities would have been lost simply because when the partners return to work without sharing, they are swamped with work and forget to refer the leads surfaced.

It is well known that professionals refer business to experts they know and like in competing firms rather than to similar experts inside their own firm, if they don't know them as well. We work hard to develop client relationships and we want the best for them when making referrals. As a result, managing partners should promote internal networking events to improve cross selling and achieve the return on investment exemplified above. *Networking internally to facilitate cross selling* is good for you too, because by creating relationship threads with your colleagues and by sharing your value propositions, you make your colleagues an extension of your sales force. They won't be selling for you but they will know to make referrals when something of value to you arises in their discussion with clients. Thank you, lawyers, for this learning.

One of the most convincing people I ever met was Tony, a short Italian New Yorker working for HP's toner division, who was brought to Asia to train the sales team in HP's sales processes. I had the pleasure to work with Tony when HP hired me to run my Star Negotiator Workshop for their team. One of the big issues needing negotiation at the time was the environmental friendliness of printer toner, that black powder that gets on your hands when you replace the toner cartridge in your printer. The environmental question had arisen a few times and the audience didn't seem convinced with the free return policy and the recycling of parts and materials that was being offered. One of the participants asked about the powder's environmental impact, so Tony jumped up, told everyone to watch, and he proceeded to open a cartridge and pour the black toner powder into his mouth. The people in the room immediately erupted in disgust and Tony made his point by swallowing the powder. Everyone was convinced; there was no problem with the toner, and the cartridge issues were dealt with. Tony's shocking demonstration of the environmental friendliness of the toner – "you can even eat it", he said with black lines streaming down his face – reminded everyone at Singapore's Grand Hyatt that *you must believe in your product, service, or idea to be convincing.* Thanks, Tony, for this great learning.

Relationships cool if not maintained. I learnt this relationship sales principle from clients that stopped hiring me, not because they didn't like my work, not because they had already run all my workshops, but simply because I didn't pay enough attention to them when my competitors did. I like to remind consultants that the moment they walk out of their client's offices, they should imagine their competitors walking in. Use your relationship threads and all other means outlined in this book to keep in touch with your clients, family, and friends, because relationships cool if not maintained. If you don't maintain your relationships, you'll find when you need these people, they no longer respond the way you might have hoped. Thank you to my former clients for this lesson.

LEARNING FROM COMPETITORS

International speakers and trainers love the questions asked by attendees because these are what keep us sharp and aware of the needs and wants of our audiences. I thank all of you for your questions. I also thank my competitors who, together with participants, force us to *continuously improve your service and quality*. The last 20 years have seen incredible change throughout the service industry, and experts that sell past solutions without continuously innovating and improving have been replaced by start-ups that arrive with new and better services, for example, Uber, Amazon, etc. If you want to succeed long-term, you need to stay alert to the trends, technological innovations, and consumer tastes. The services you sold may no longer be needed or maybe you need to sell them in a different way. Your ideas might have been needed then but no longer respond to the current situation. I was needed as a paper boy, then as a camp counsellor, then as an auditor, then as head of learning and development, then as a trainer, and now as a master trainer, speaker, and author. If I was still trying to sell newspapers, I certainly wouldn't be where I am now. Change is constant, so your services (and quality) should be continuously improving too. Thank you to my competitors for continuously pushing the envelope.

SELF-LEARNING

I have learnt a lot from others, but I've also found it useful to reflect on what has gone well, what has gone less well, and why. Reflective practitioners are people who work like everyone else but pause periodically to reflect on how to improve what they do and how they do it. If you are reading this book, you are likely a reflective practitioner. Use your time between meetings to reflect and note what you have learnt, to think about what was done well and what can be improved. This simple practice differentiates highly successful leaders from the rest. Become a reflective practitioner.

I count five relationship sales principles as arising out of my self-reflection. The first of these is one that causes gasps when people hear it and is a great performance measure for anyone wanting to succeed in the business of sales. *Sales are based on dialogues and dialogues are based on relationships.* How many dialogues should we have each day to succeed? The magic number is five. Typically, this means two in each of the morning and afternoon and one at lunch. The dialogue should be sufficient to uncover or strengthen relationship threads, or to Ma-Ma the needs or wants of the other party. The contact can take place on the telephone, video conference, face to face or via text messaging, but in person is always best. If you want to generate leads and fill your Bulldog Opportunity Tracker, *make five contacts per day, 25 contacts per week, 100 contacts per month, 1200 contacts per year.* Most people are aghast when this expectation is held over them, but when you do it yourself, you will find it very useful as a marker reminding you that you can't fill your sales pipeline if you are not talking to your target audience. Just do it. This is an average. I have days when I have many more than five dialogues and then I have other days when I have only a couple of dialogues. I have days when one dialogue brings business and others when five dialogues bring no leads. The essence here is to sustain the momentum, because if you are having a thousand dialogues a year, you will sell, learn why you are not selling, understand how to influence others, learn how to sell yourself. The solution is in the dialogue, but just like training for a marathon, you need to put in the miles, if you want to win the dialogue sales process, you need to engage in a sufficient number of dialogues.

When you dialogue with others, *don't focus on yourself, focus on the other person.* Ask questions about them, bring Ma-Ma to the table, sustain the focus on them and their answers. Resist the temptation to talk about yourself, your value propositions, your amazing experience and credentials. You know about yourself but you don't know about them. You need to consciously focus on them, otherwise you won't uncover their relationship threads, needs, wants, and motivational dialect. Once you know these, you can adopt their motivational dialect and share how your value propositions can help address their needs, wants, etc. If you want to practice, I recommend you do this with a friend and ask them to signal to you every time you bring the conversation back onto yourself. People who struggle to talk about anyone but themselves aren't very good in dialogue and don't demonstrate much care in others. If you have a bit of this tendency, practice consciously to focus on the needs of the other party and you will find friendships improve, you learn a lot more than you ever knew, and solutions emerge from your dialogue.

If you are regularly engaging in five contacts a day and bringing Ma-Ma to the table, focusing your dialogue on the other party, you will quickly begin surfacing the needs and wants of the people you are talking to. The next relationship selling principle is therefore to *respond to the needs and wants of others regardless of payback*. Firstly, if you help others they will want to help you. Secondly, if you help others altruistically (regardless of payback), you will stand out in their mind as being very kind. Kindness helps strengthen relationship threads and because we are human, when we help others they want to help us. Some call this karma. I realise that the more you give, the more you receive. That is why I give a lot of my time to not-for-profit organisations, accept to speak even if the audience falls below expected levels, and give away my knowledge in the form of books, apps etc. Give and thou shalt receive is ancient wisdom, but in today's sharing economy it is more relevant than ever before.

Every contact you make with someone should result in you knowing more about their needs, wants, relationship threads, and motivations. Every dialogue you undertake should also leave them clearer about the value you can bring to their situation and how to reach you should they be interested. One of the best lessons I've learnt is to *give people something to remember you*. In addition to my business card, I normally give memory joggers, pocket cards, playing cards, games, apps, books, links to videos etc. Everything I give is a reminder of what I do and how to reach me. I won business once in Australia and asked the client how he found me. He said he couldn't remember my name but he had a copy of my book and that's where he found my email address.

The final relationship sales principle is perhaps the one that I think of the most and it comes in part from my respect for Winston Churchill who reminded his nation to "never, never, never give up". My version of this is *persist, persist, persist*. Since I started my business, I have faced an endless series of setbacks, but because I persist through all the challenges, I have succeeded to build the consultancy I imagined when I started out. You will certainly face setbacks and some will seem insurmountable. Remember, it is always darkest before the dawn. Remember, rainbows require a storm and diamonds result from pressure. If you want to succeed, persist, persist, persist.

The relationship selling principles listed above were discovered either from family, colleagues, thought leaders, industry, or self-reflection. Here,

I classify my relationship sales principles into three groups, each named with a Sanskrit word.

The first group, I name the Indra group, in recognition of Indra's Net, an ancient Hindu concept that we are all interconnected like in a cobweb, so our actions must consider everyone else in the web. Change leaders sometimes get frustrated when their plans face resistance from others, but once they recognise they too are part of Indra's Net, they will place more importance on dialogue with other stakeholders about whatever it is they are trying to sell. *We are all connected whether we like to believe it, or not.* We cannot build walls to divide us because walls wither. Relationship threads continue through generations.

I name the second group of relationship selling principles Karma. Karma is a Sanskrit term which suggests *our future is a direct result of our intent and actions in the present.* Whereas the first group reminds us of the importance of relationships, the second group reminds us of the importance of behaviour.

The third category of relationship selling principles, I call Mandala, again a Sanskrit term, this time referring to the activity of focusing attention by making a representation of the universe, sometimes using coloured sand crystals, which upon completion, are brushed away destroying the mandala and reminding the creators of the impermanence of everything. *This group reminds us of the need to sustain our efforts over time if we are to achieve results.*

Relationship Sales Principles by Group

The Indra Group of Relationship Sales Principles (selling = relationships)

1. You don't have clients you have relationships.
2. Relationships cool if not maintained.
3. Never cease to develop relationships.
4. Some clients can't say yes but don't want to say no.
5. Interrupt relationship building to do your work.
6. Say thank you.
7. Keep your word.

The Karma Group of relationship sales principles (selling = behaviour)

8. Help the buyer to say no if you realise they can't say yes.
9. Network internally to facilitate cross selling.

10. Don't focus on yourself, focus on the other party.
11. Ask lots of questions to surface unstated needs.
12. Keep building your SECS Appeal.
13. Give client something to remember you.
14. Reward those who refer you (appropriately).

The Mandala Group of relationship sales principles (selling = persistence)

15. Make 5 contacts/day, 25/week, 100/month, 1200/year.
16. Respond to the needs of others, regardless of feedback.
17. Ask for business and ask for referral.
18. Continuously improve your service and quality.
19. Learn all about your competitors.
20. Become knowledgeable of all related prices.
21. Persist, persist, persist.

4

A Business Developer's Workday

Working as an auditor in an international audit firm takes a lot of getting used to, but after ten years I was very much at home in the high-pressure, high-performance environment. I was a senior manager knocking on the door of partnership and I lived the culture as much as anyone. When the firm reneged on their agreement to make me a profit centre I decided to leave the firm rather than put an end to our plans of building a change management consultancy. Instead of starting the practice inside the firm I would simply work from home and engage my UK partners whenever I won business. The change from working in a big firm to working at home was enormous. Gone were the structure, the support, the colleagues, the fun. In addition to finding, doing, and billing for my work, I was also now responsible for accounts receivable, IT, garbage, tea, cleaning, etc.

If you are contemplating a similar change in your life or if you have made the leap to being self-employed, here are the ten elements I put into my daily routine which contributed to my success. I do (most of) these things daily regardless of where I am working in the world. I am on the road roughly one week per month, so travel is a regular aspect of my life. Having a routine while the rest of the world changes around you is an important element of success. Since my suitcase is always either being emptied, filled, or transported, having a routine has proven to be very helpful.

When you rent a vehicle, you can drive just about any make of car or truck because the dashboard, steering, gas, brake, and signal lights are mostly standardised across automotive brands. Whenever you sit at a desk or table to work or learn you should be similarly well organised. Here is what you need to have in place to be successful.

SET UP YOUR COCKPIT AND DASHBOARD

I carry a diary with me whenever I go to meetings. In my diary, I have an 18-month at-a-glance calendar to plan and keep track of my appointments. I have a "3 days per page" section where I note appointments and track my daily "To Do" list. I have a section for note taking (kept chronologically), one for telephone calls, and one for client meetings and thinking sessions. The note pages are later removed and put into client files which I use to keep track of client engagements. My diary also includes my Bulldog Opportunity Tracker and my monthly timesheet. In addition to my diary I also have my travel file, in-tray file, and client files as required. I always have my smartphone and charger and I carry all of this in different bags according to my daily needs. These things are pretty much always with me and together with my PC they create my cockpit and dashboard from which I tackle my daily To Do list, anytime, anywhere.

THINK CLEARLY

It might seem silly to even have to mention it, but you have to be fully present and have your ideas logically ordered if you are meeting clients. Sometimes clients are confused, and if they notice you are confused it is unlikely you will ever win work, let alone do a good job. Use relationship threads and the value proposition template to help order your thoughts. Get used to using mind maps, challenge maps, and methodologies like the power of three, or Think on your Feet®, to order your logic and help your clients think straight. Once you help your clients think better, you are well on your way to winning business from them.

DIALOGUE FIVE TIMES PER DAY

Your workday is incomplete if you haven't called or met with at least five people a day, 25 a week, 100 a month, 1,200 a year, to surface needs, wants, relationship threads, motivational dialect, etc. If your daily schedule doesn't include networking, make sure you don't miss more than a few days a week; otherwise you simply won't be meeting enough people or having enough conversations to fill your sales pipeline and sell yourself, your ideas, or your services.

MAKE YOUR SALES CALLS EFFECTIVE

When I started out no one told me how to conduct sales calls. I wasn't very good at all in the beginning but in time I became very good at it. When I was new to sales calls I emphasised preparation but now I emphasise presence. Give yourself at least two hours for each meeting, arrive with a blank sheet of paper, bring Ma-Ma to the table, and ask lots of questions, watching the body language as you go. It is great to think in advance about what questions you want to ask and what questions you think they will ask you. Plan for the hardest questions but don't prepare too much. Go prepared to listen and to be surprised because things change constantly and what you thought might be the case may not be what you end up hearing. Good meetings might last 90 minutes. The extra half-hour is for you to make notes and get to your next meeting on time. If the meeting finishes earlier you have more time to make notes, make calls, and get to your next meeting. Book your client meetings starting at the end of the week and work back to Monday. In this way, you will maximise your time management. Book calls in the same part of town so you don't waste time in travel.

PROVIDE GREAT SERVICE

You will never return to a bad restaurant, but you will likely tell all your friends about your bad experience. Likewise, when someone really impresses you, you tend to want to tell others. Your best sales technique will be great service. If you are selling yourself or your ideas, leave others liking you and wanting to work with you. If they don't have a pleasant experience speaking with you, they are unlikely to hire you, agree to your ideas, or buy your services.

COLLECT AND RESPOND TO FEEDBACK

You should seek out feedback on a daily basis, because, like waves brushing against broken glass on a beach, the only way you will become smooth and attractive to others is if you ask for and respond to feedback on a regular basis. Just think about people you find odd, either in dress, thoughts, or behaviour. These people are typically those who have the least feedback from others and/or choose to not respond accordingly. Outliers have different ideas to other people but to get other people to accept you, your ideas, or your services, you need others to like you and to want to work with you. Asking for and responding to feedback will enable you to tweak your presentation, ideas, or services to become more attractive to others. Without getting feedback and responding accordingly you won't have much luck being hired or followed by others. What sort of feedback should you be asking for? Three questions are all it takes. Be sure to discuss both what you do and how you do it.

1. What have I done well?
2. What can I improve?
3. Any other comments?

JUGGLE SEVERAL THINGS AT ONCE

Everyone trying to change the world knows you have to juggle a lot of things at the same time. On any given day, you might be doing client work, collecting debtors, sending invoices, doing sales calls, meeting family responsibilities, getting some exercise, doing administration, managing staff, getting some sleep. You'd better be having fun because days like this can go on forever. Your ability to juggle several things at once will either become one of your skills or cause your downfall. There is seldom a perfect day to do just one thing and so the better you become at juggling several things in the same day, the better off you will be. You cannot afford to wait for that perfect day to do just one thing. You need to keep them all moving at the same time.

TAKE TIME TO REFLECT EACH DAY

Your day must include some quiet time where you reflect on the time just past and the time to come so that you can make sense of the past and begin to shape the future. Failure to take time out for reflection means you are simply reacting to whatever happens along the way. Like a captain that plans a trip before setting sail, your reflection time is needed to assess where you have come and where you want to go next. It is also a time to recharge your batteries, equally as valuable as sleep. My friend Denis who runs his own business in Vancouver and has several employees likes to call it "unavailable time" when his clients and staff call and his secretary says "Sorry, Denis is not currently available". Staff solve their problems without him, clients call their account managers, and Denis has the time he needs for personal reflection. You can't run a business without personal reflection time. Ask any successful executive.

CONTINUOUSLY IMPROVE YOUR DIALOGUE AND NEGOTIATION SKILLS

The two essential skills for successfully selling yourself, your ideas, or your professional services are to dialogue and negotiate successfully. Successful dialogue includes preparing the dialogue puzzle (stakeholders, issues, process, outcome), sharpening your dialogue skills (presence, respect, expression, suspending, absorbing), and leveraging different dialogue methods. These things are explained in my book *Dialogue Gap* so I won't repeat details here, but suffice it to say, you can't sell if you can't dialogue and no one will entrust their future to you, your ideas, or your services if they don't feel comfortable with you in dialogue. Similarly, you are unlikely to ever get 100% of what you want so you need to learn to negotiate. I describe the negotiation process and skills in my book *Negotiation: Mastering Business in Asia*. Star Negotiators are good at every step in the negotiation process (preparation, introduction, objection, creation, and documentation) and employ skills to get what they deserve (dialogue, tactics, information, people, situation). If you want to be good at selling yourself, your ideas, or your professional services, you need to be good and getting better, because the buyers you are talking to are getting better all the time too.

LOOK AFTER YOURSELF

Selling is physically, mentally, and spiritually exhausting so be sure to look after yourself to ensure you remain in good shape despite the highs and lows that come with selling yourself, your ideas, or your services. When selling succeeds you are on a high but when you fail you can get depressed. Be sure to rest, exercise regularly, eat properly, avoid alcohol and drugs, listen to music, laugh, smell the flowers, read a book, spend time with family and friends, and return to work 100% charged up to conquer another day.

You can also recharge your battery by meditating on compassion or praying for those people who stand between you and your goals. Think about what causes these people to think the way they do and often you'll find yourself feeling compassion for how sad other aspects of their lives must be if they think the way they do. Seeking compassion for your enemies will also give you inspiration to dialogue and negotiate with them in new ways that just might convince them. At least if you show compassion they will tend to like you more (or dislike you less) and, as I said before, this can't be a bad thing when it comes to getting what you want.

It might be hard to have a perfect day, but you can have a perfect week, and you can balance things out over time – so play the long game, do the things I've outlined above, and aim to make every day a great day.

5

Other Important Sales Topics

ONLINE SELLING

Selling yourself, your ideas, and your services online provides an amazing opportunity for people today. Think about how much you buy today using eBay, Amazon, Uber, or other in-app or e-shop stores. If you are selling yourself, LinkedIn replacing traditional CVs and portfolios are now presented on YouTube. While these services facilitate sharing details with prospective employers or buyers, the internet also shares information that might kill your sale. Google your name and check what comes up. Click on images and videos. Is your online presence helping or hindering your sales efforts?

Selling ideas and services online requires more work than selling yourself. If you want to leverage the web to sell your ideas and services, you need to be posting information and growing your footprint all the time. Try to build up a following by friending everyone in your network and targeting individuals with big followings (e.g. thought leaders in your area of expertise). The more you post, tweet, share, the more you grow your presence. I must stress this is addictive and might leave you feeling like you are selling, but really you are marketing (getting yourself known). If you are alone in front of your computer, you aren't engaging in dialogue with five contacts per day, 25 per week, 100 per month, 1,200 per year, which means you aren't filling your Bulldog Opportunity Tracker. I need to constantly remind myself to balance my time online with time face to face with prospective clients. That said, LinkedIn, Facebook, Twitter, Messenger, We Chat, Instagram, WhatsApp, and traditional email are all great tools for reminding people of your presence and value add, as well as for keeping in touch with your key contacts. Be sure to identify which channel your key contacts prefer so you can follow up their relationship threads using their preferred medium.

SOFTWARE SOLUTIONS

Salesforce, apps, blogs, digital newsletter services, and other online tools are also greatly assisting your sales efforts today. Don't underestimate the time and expertise it takes to manage these tools. Consider recruiting help to manage these while you focus on selling and service delivery. I have had limited success with my app because I failed to recognise the challenge to market it, maintain it, and monetise it. Read all you can about doing apps successfully (I recommend *How to Build a Billion-Dollar App* by George Berkowski [Piatkus, 2014]). Most of the things that can go wrong will and I am reminded that only 10% of apps succeed, if that.

I don't use Salesforce or other CRM software because I don't believe it is necessary for a small business like mine where I know all my clients personally. I don't blog because I prefer speaking and writing books, but if you like to blog you should do so weekly and use multimedia to attract as much interest as possible. Keep track of the stats on your blog and assess your return on investment. If no one is reading your blog, ask yourself if it is the best use of your time.

I like my digital newsletter service because it allows me to write a targeted message and send it to my entire database (currently in the thousands) as well as to my Facebook, Twitter, and LinkedIn followers. I like the fact my followers can repost my newsletters to their followers and I like the fact it includes links to my app, e-shop, public workshops, etc. If your newsletter service isn't linked to social media, it is time to switch. I use Constant Contact which is okay for my needs. One important question to resolve is how you will manage your contact database or address book. It is near impossible to keep this up to date, and unless it is automated you will find yourself struggling to find people wanting to work on this for you. Ensure your website, app, blog, social media, and digital newsletters include an option to sign up for future notifications. It is all about growing your footprint and once you open the door to this, you will no longer know everyone in your database. Do what you can to protect your data and prevent hackers from accessing your address book. Keep your internet security software up to date. Hire help when you need it. Your time is best devoted to selling yourself, your ideas, and your services, not fixing computers and wasting time on software.

Keep your website simple and follow current best practices. Remember that software is constantly upgrading, so you'll need to maintain your website. Use video, offer links to your social media pages, and promote specific calls to action for visitors to your site such as subscribing to your newsletter, signing up for workshops, purchasing from your e-shop, contacting you, and making referrals.

BIG DATA

If your ideas or services call for collection of intelligence, consider the commercial opportunities available to you by using your network to collect data. If you collect enough valuable data, then you can monetise this and turn it into another service line. To help people negotiate complex negotiations I developed the NegotiatorCPA negotiation preparation app. Every time a negotiator enters their data to produce terms sheets for their negotiation they also give me the opportunity to leverage their data (anonymously) to further help people with similar negotiations. In other words, the more you know the more you can help, and the more you help the more you will know. Consider how to create such a system for your service line and leverage what is presently one of the best opportunities available to service professionals and thought leaders.

A WORD FOR BUYERS

The sales process and the procurement process are two sides of the same table. Seated across from every seller is a buyer and vice versa. I have trained a lot of buyers to achieve greater value for money from the procurement process. Buyers often feel outsmarted by sales professionals, who typically know more than buyers about the market, prices, competitors, and options available to save money or increase return on investment. The secret to being a better buyer is learning to be a better seller. This book is equally for buyers and sellers, two sides of the same table. As my DNA double helix icon signifies, sometimes the seller is on top and sometimes the buyer is on top, but both are connected through the five steps of the process: plan, connect, dialogue, record, and follow up.

One of the best books I have read on professional services was written by David Maister, entitled *Managing the Professional Service Firm* (Free

Press, 1993). In his book Maister identifies nine criteria which buyers use when choosing their professional advisors. These are:

1. How prepared are you?
2. Don't expect me to acknowledge need/problem/opportunity.
3. Give me an education.
4. How you speak tells me how you will treat me as client.
5. Be sympathetic of my role.
6. Share your experience on the problems you know I have.
7. Convince me my need is big enough to bother doing something about.
8. If I'm still interested, tell me how you can help me.
9. Even if I ask for a proposal, recognise that trust demonstrated face to face is most important.

The list is self-explanatory and if you want further details I encourage you to read the book. The three things that stand out for me on the above list are (one) recognising you should not try to sell until you get to step eight, everything up to that point is dialogue. The second thing is to recognise that sometimes the buyer is responsible for the problem causing the need for your professional services in which case compassion is probably your best response. Thirdly is Maister's reminder that how you talk to your buyer face to face is of paramount importance in giving the buyer comfort to buy your services. If you are a buyer, and you are not being treated well by the person trying to sell you their ideas or services, then I encourage you to call them out on it or put an end to the discussion right away. Don't allow yourself to be taken in by an aggressive results-oriented individual who doesn't demonstrate care for you and your situation. You can let someone else satisfy this vendor's monthly sales quota. Life is too short to waste time with people who don't care about you.

SALES DIALOGUES – TIPS FROM *DIALOGUE GAP*

Not everyone reading this book will be able to spend time reading the dialogue skills and methods outlined in my book *Dialogue Gap*. If you are trying to sell yourself, your ideas, or your services, then you need to be good at dialogue. Here are things you need to know.

Planning your dialogue is very important for success. To achieve an optimal outcome, you need the right people, to discuss the right issues, in the right way, time, and space. I call this the dialogue puzzle and describe each piece of the puzzle in my book. If you are trying to sell yourself, your ideas, or your services, you need to determine what an optimal outcome will look like, identify who the key people are in your situation, identify the dozens of issues related to your situation, and decide the process (way, time, space) needed to achieve your optimal outcome.

One of the key elements of choosing the right way is knowing dialogue skills. I have identified 50 such skills, all of which are described in my book. There are five categories of ten skills each. The categories include the following:

- Being fully present and mindful while in dialogue to recognise everything spoken and unspoken
- Being respectful without which others will not open to you preventing you from making your sale
- Express yourself and help others do the same so you can deal with the issues as they surface
- Suspend your thoughts and emotions to create space into which the perspectives, thoughts, and feelings of others can percolate into your conscious
- Absorb the spoken and unspoken messages being sent and received through the dialogue to validate what you think to be going on

In addition to the dialogue puzzle and dialogue skills, there are also dozens of dialogue methods available for use in your situation. Choosing a method useful for your situation is much better than choosing one that doesn't work. If you think how much people open up to you when they are alone with you versus how their behaviour changes when they are in public, you realise how changing the method, time, and space will impact your desired outcome. In *Dialogue Gap*, I outline some 50 different dialogue methods, all of which are useful but some of which are more useful than others given the size of the group, the presence of conflict, the need for ideas, the need for engagement, etc.

SALES NEGOTIATIONS – TIPS FROM *NEGOTIATION: MASTERING BUSINESS IN ASIA*

Not everyone reading this book will be able to spend time reading about the negotiation skills and tactics outlined in my book *Negotiation: Mastering Business in Asia*. However, if you are trying to negotiate yourself into a job or negotiate adoption of your ideas or services, then you need to be a good negotiator.

I list below the 20 most common negotiation mistakes that I see people making when trying to negotiate for jobs, ideas, or services. I discuss these problems in my negotiation book together with what to do at each stage of the negotiation process and how to emulate the attributes of Star Negotiators. Since your time is limited here's what you need to know about the three biggest challenges on the list.

Preparation

The biggest challenge is that people don't sufficiently prepare before trying to sell themselves, their ideas, or their services. There is never enough time to prepare but it is important to make best use of the time you do have to get as ready as possible for the negotiation. There are three things you need to prepare (content, process, people). In terms of content you need to know the issues, for example, if you are selling yourself you need to know the range for salary, compensation, benefits, timing, competition, expertise, job requirements, etc. In terms of process, you need to understand you are entering a negotiation and you won't get everything you want. You need to prepare your concessions ("If I do this, then will you do that") and tactics to get what you want. It is even useful to practise before engaging in the real negotiation. In terms of people, you need to identify the key stakeholders and understand their motivational threads, needs, and wants as described earlier. You should prepare to change your dialect to better connect with and influence the people in your situation.

Learning

The second most common problem that I've seen in negotiation is that people underestimate the amount of learning needed before it is possible to visualise and achieve an optimal outcome. Through dialogue people learn the issues and each other's needs, wants, and motivations. If, however, people begin negotiating thinking they know it all, make firm statements, and persist in their position wanting the other party to concede, they will not create the space needed for learning so the chance of achieving an optimal outcome is eliminated, and conflict will arise. Just look around the world at present trade, environment, and peace negotiations and you'll see what I'm referring to. *Negotiation is a learning process. The solution is in the dialogue.*

Emotions

We can all think of situations where we lost control of our emotions when trying to convince someone of something. We feel frustration when people don't appear to care about us, our ideas, or our services. We feel used when people take advantage of us. We shrink in our self-esteem when passed over in favour of others when selling ourselves, our ideas, or our services. We fight or flee conflict even though we know we should keep our cool and continue dialogue. Emotional control is one of the signs of a good negotiator. There are three things I recommend if you want to improve your emotional control.

First is to know yourself better. Each of us is programmed to react in a predictable way when under stress or faced with conflict. In my workshops, you learn your conflict sequence and how to de-escalate stress and conflict to return to dialogue in hope of achieving optimal outcomes. Your conflict sequence is diagnosed using dialogue and a motivational assessment. When pushed to our limit in conflictual or stressful situations we predictably pass through three motivational styles. Most people react to conflict by stopping in their tracks and assessing the danger. Sometimes this allows them to think of a solution and the conflict dissipates. If the conflict escalates, people change their behaviour and most try being nice. Again, if this works, great, and if not and the problem escalates again, people jump into action. While this is the most common reaction it might not be yours and it might not be the best sequence to react in your situation. Sometimes starting with being nice or jumping to action is what's needed. Knowing yourself is very important because if you don't know your natural reaction, you won't be able to assess if another reaction is warranted.

The second thing you can do to better control your emotions is to have compassion for the other party that is causing you to lose your equanimity. I've had thousands of people tell me their negotiations are going wrong and that they really don't like the other person. When I ask about the other person's wants, needs, or motivations, the common retort is "who cares, they're an ***hole". I totally understand this reaction and it is normal to feel this way but it isn't the best way to feel if you want to resolve the conflict and achieve an optimal outcome. Instead, what I recommend is to find compassion for the other party. For example, a client of mine was very upset one of their suppliers was late delivering on an important project. As a result, my client cut the supplier from the next round of tenders. Rather than have compassion for why they were late and engage in dialogue to learn about the issues, they simply shut them out of their next tender and ended up giving the next contract to a competing supplier. When the second supplier was also late on delivery my client got even more upset. When I encouraged them to have compassion for the supplier's having to pay penalties for late delivery and to dialogue to uncover the problem, they found out the delay was due to a shortage of talent in the industry facing all the suppliers, not just the ones my client had engaged. My client wanted to achieve an optimal outcome, but only once compassion led to dialogue did they find out the underlying problem and find a workaround to complete their two projects on time.

The third thing I recommend for keeping your emotions in check is what I've noticed all great leaders do on a regular basis. To maintain your equanimity in the face of the endless problems that come with trying to sell yourself, your ideas, or your professional services, your daily routine needs to include quality exercise, sleep, and diet as well as a daily quiet time (e.g. nature walk, meditation, prayer, reading, music, repetitive exercise, etc.) to allow your head, heart, and soul to return to their natural settled state. Find what works for you and as you get busier you should be taking short time-outs more often. If not, you'll be reacting without the emotional control you need to achieve an optimal outcome.

MOST COMMON NEGOTIATION MISTAKES

Appendix X shows the top 20 negotiation mistakes.

CONFLICT

You can't sell yourself, your ideas, or your services without someday facing conflict of some kind. I discussed above three ways to "keep your head when all about you are losing theirs and blaming it on you". These are ways to control your emotions when your reptilian brain simply tells you to get rid of your opponents. Competition is a natural part of the selling process and it is natural for conflicts to erupt from time to time. We want to win a job but others might go behind our back to favour themselves or their friends. We want to sell our ideas but others will pick holes in our arguments. We want to sell our services but our competitors highlight our weaknesses. We want clients to pay and keep their word but they interpret the situation differently and don't want to pay as much, on time, or at all. *Conflict is part of the game and if you want to succeed in selling living solutions you also need to be good at conflict resolution.* There are 40 strategies listed below to help you reduce stress, resolve conflict, return to dialogue, and achieve optimal outcomes. Here are three strategies I find particularly useful (Appendix VI).

CONFLICT DE-ESCALATION TACTICS

Appendix VI shows de-escalation tactics.

Change Time or Space

A lot of conflict results from deadlines imposed by one party to cut short dialogue and force a decision. If this is your situation, take time to quantify the value lost when an optimal outcome is not achieved and try using this to create an incentive for removing the deadline and resuming dialogue. Sometimes the space in which you are holding your negotiation is contributing to the stress. Consider changing the location to achieve a more harmonious outcome. Simply taking a time-out is often one of the best things you can do, but be sure to resume dialogue so that time-outs don't become avoidance.

Create Choice

Often conflict arises in situations where one party is bullying another. If you remove one of the two parties the conflict extinguishes itself. If you are in this type of situation give yourself a choice. Try selling to or buying from someone else. In job situations finding another employer or division of the company might be a better option than continuing to deal with the conflict you are facing at present. If your ideas are creating conflict you have a choice to stop selling your ideas or to start selling your ideas to someone else. If your professional services have resulted in conflict you too can choose your clients. When you are starting out you feel you need every client but as you become better at selling you quickly realise wasting time in conflict with one client is very costly in terms of keeping you from working with other clients that will bring you much more value.

Persist with Compassion

The third strategy I have found particularly effective for people trying to sell themselves, their ideas, or their services is to dig in your heels, show compassion for the buyer's needs, let them realise you are here to help them, and remind the buyer that you are not going away until they say yes. This is a favoured strategy of one of my good friends, Mark Saykaly. Mark learnt this strategy running his family business and he now employs it to bring positive change to two leading not-for-profit organisations that he is helping govern.

In the face of unrelenting persistence smothered with kindness a lot of people end up saying yes. I have found that most people concede and agree if you persist at least three times. Difficult situations might require considerable persistence to win over the other side. *If you believe in what you are doing and genuinely care about the other side, it won't be hard for you to persist.* In time, you will get what you want or learn how to adjust your offering for the other side to ultimately say yes.

SELLING ACROSS CULTURES – TIPS FROM *CORPORATE CULTURE*

In my book *Corporate Culture: Hurdles to Being #1 in the Private and Public Sectors Today,* I identify nine cultural differences separating

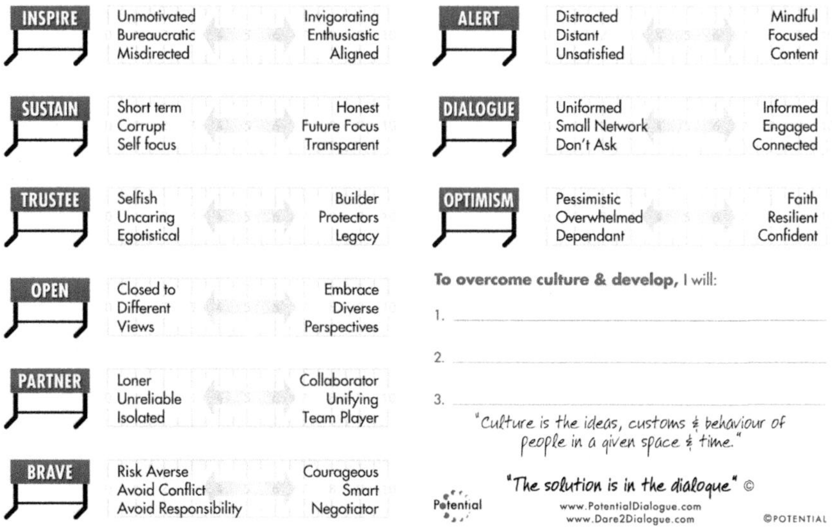

INSPIRE	Unmotivated	Invigorating		ALERT	Distracted	Mindful
	Bureaucratic	Enthusiastic			Distant	Focused
	Misdirected	Aligned			Unsatisfied	Content

SUSTAIN	Short term	Honest		DIALOGUE	Uniformed	Informed
	Corrupt	Future Focus			Small Network	Engaged
	Self focus	Transparent			Don't Ask	Connected

TRUSTEE	Selfish	Builder		OPTIMISM	Pessimistic	Faith
	Uncaring	Protectors			Overwhelmed	Resilient
	Egotistical	Legacy			Dependant	Confident

OPEN	Closed to	Embrace
	Different	Diverse
	Views	Perspectives

To overcome culture & develop, I will:

1. _____

2. _____

3. _____

PARTNER	Loner	Collaborator
	Unreliable	Unifying
	Isolated	Team Player

"Culture is the ideas, customs & behaviour of people in a given space & time."

BRAVE	Risk Averse	Courageous
	Avoid Conflict	Smart
	Avoid Responsibility	Negotiator

"The solution is in the dialogue." ©

Potential
www.PotentialDialogue.com
www.Dare2Dialogue.com
©POTENTIAL

FIGURE 5.1
Cultural Hurdles separating twenty-first-century winners from also-rans.

winning leaders and organisations from their also-rans. Cultural hurdles are behaviours that winners do consistently well but which others stumble upon or get stopped by in pursuit of their goals. If you are selling yourself, your ideas, or your services to the winning leaders and organisations that have learnt to overcome these cultural hurdles, you must ensure your solutions consider these cultural hurdles to ensure the buyer sees you as a potential solution provider. The nine cultural hurdles are listed above (Figure 5.1). Here are three examples explaining how to effectively sell yourself, your ideas, or your services to winning leaders and organisations.

Selling Yourself

I am grateful for the opportunity to work with leading organisations around the world. I've witnessed the profound differences between the winners and the also-rans. The best organisations have very talented people who collaborate and innovate to bring leading solutions to their clients. They have fun at work, stimulate each other towards achieving better results and support each other when the going gets tough. Individually these organisations don't necessarily have the top talent in their industry but they do have the best teams. As the saying goes, "no one is perfect but a team can be". If you want to join one of these leading private or public sector organisations you must prove you have the talent they need (the whole world wants to work for them), you must show you are already a leader in whatever you are doing, and that you will be a positive contribution to their team motivating others on the team who want to work with you and vice versa. If you don't think you are ready to sell yourself at this level it is better to wait and develop yourself rather than try but fail. These winning organisations seldom look at candidates more than once.

Selling Your Ideas

Leading thinkers and service providers regularly approach winning organisations globally. Winning organisations search for talent and thought leaders throughout the world and pay handsomely to get what they want. This is your competition so if you want to sell your ideas in the international arena you need to have great ideas and sell them better than anyone else. You don't have to be from New York, London, or Hong Kong, but you do need to know how to compete with world leaders from leading international markets. Here are three tips to help you succeed. *Firstly, don't assume you are the only one to have your idea.* People travel and the internet has levelled the playing field. It isn't about having a unique idea, it has more to do with making your idea work in the local context. Skype came from Tallinn, Estonia, a tiny nation on the Baltic. Cirque de Soleil came from Quebec. Nokia came from Finland. Blackberry came from Ottawa. Often great ideas come from small communities replete with friends, dialogue, and a cost base that provides time to create. *Secondly, remember that great ideas grow viral from a strong base,* so build your base before spreading your wings. Buyers look to whence you came and if they find excited committed followers in your market it is a positive influence. If they find you to be unknown even at home, it makes your sales efforts that much harder. Let the international success come after building your base locally. *Thirdly, recognise your ideas will meet more opposition the more successful you become.* When Microsoft Excel and Word took over the office software market in the 1990s, there were still local holdouts pushing for Lotus 1-2-3 and WordPerfect, which were the leading spreadsheet and word processing software at the time. Despite the obvious takeover of MS Office, opposition to its adoption was fierce because it meant the IT people who promoted Lotus and WordPerfect had to admit defeat and accept that their idea of the best office software had been wrong. Be prepared for tough competition as you take your ideas further afield. Your friends will be less prominent and your enemies more prepared to make their presence known. Consider using some of the 200+ tactics shared in *Negotiation: Mastering Business in Asia.*

To sell your ideas across cultures, don't just consider the culture of winning organisations, also consider how the local ethnic culture and religious norms will respond to your ideas. Go local, talk to people, ask for their candid feedback *before* investing great sums of money or time in a new market, especially one you don't know much about. I have watched many American and European companies fail in Asia simply because they thought what worked in their culture would work in Asia. Sometimes the ideas only need tweaking to succeed. Sometimes they need to be marketed in a different way. Sometimes originals have to accept their ideas simply aren't going to work in Asia. Global companies now split their businesses into three to four geographic divisions, recognising that what works in the Americas might not work in Europe, Africa, or Asia. Ideas, like products, should be tested before being sold. Sellers of ideas should test-drive their ideas in new markets to understand what challenges they will face in the adoption of their ideas. Talk to the people in the local markets; the solution is in the dialogue.

Selling Professional Services

Selling professional services in a different culture results in more challenges then selling yourself or your ideas (Figure 5.1). I have helped a lot of executives sell into new markets. To succeed, you and your colleagues need to be good at all the dialogue selling best practices and relationship selling principles, but you also need to realise success in a new culture will take a lot of time, money, and dialogue to learn how to compete and win. Meanwhile, as your firm tries to succeed, your professionals will be enjoying the trips and experiences the new culture offers while also making cultural missteps, missing their family and friends back home, and wondering how much longer they will need to stay in the new culture before going home. *Foreigners will want to return home earlier than it will take for them to really make it big in the new culture.* In Hong Kong, people say foreigners stay for one, three, or five years, or forever. I arrived on an 18-month contract and have stayed nearly 30 years. In the meantime, Canada has changed a lot and returning home would require as much of an adjustment as moving to a new market. If you want to sell into a new culture, be humble, accept there is a lot you don't know, and recognise it might be three years before you begin to understand what is really going on. Up to that point you will be only scratching the surface of understanding. You might have initial success, but really success in new cultures takes time. The rewards of working in new cultures are significant both personally and professionally. Once you have learnt to succeed in two new cultures you will begin to find the learning process in new cultures becomes a lot easier. When I moved from Canada to Switzerland I faced a big learning curve. When I moved from Switzerland to Hong Kong the learning curve was just as big, but several of the issues I had seen once before. Now that I have worked successfully in nearly 60 countries around the world, I have come to find the adaptation a whole lot easier. Stepping into a new culture today isn't really any different than my first few steps into Europe or Asia years ago. What has changed is my acceptance of what is considered normal in one culture might be completely different in another. Becoming comfortable in a multicultural world is a privilege offered to the adventurous, those willing to subject themselves to stepping out of their comfort zone, dealing with the ridicule involved in learning new cultures, and missing home. *In today's globalised world, being comfortable selling yourself globally is much better than remaining local and fearful of the encroaching cultures which are changing the face of our communities forever.* Good luck. Remember, the solution is in the dialogue.

6

Conclusion

I attended a LinkedIn seminar recently which espoused the differences between high-tech and high-touch. While it is true that social selling is opening doors like never before, the importance of dialogue selling will never be replaced by LinkedIn or any other form of social media. People need to understand each other, trust each other, and have some form of a relationship before they accept to do business together.

Social selling might help open doors but when you are face to face with a potential client, it is your ability to leverage the dialogue selling process and relationship selling principles outlined in this playbook that will enable you to scope, win, and deliver business better than anyone else – including your competitors, who might have more followers than you. If you don't believe me, just ask anyone you know that met a significant other via the web. What was more important, the computer-generated connection or the ensuing face-to-face dialogue? The reality is longstanding rewarding relationships need both effective computer-assisted connections and face-to-face dialogue.

In this book, I've helped you recognise and learn key steps in the dialogue selling process as well as the background and reasoning supporting the relationship selling principles. Each situation you face will start at a different place in the process and some situations will rely more on certain principles than others. Having a clear understanding of the process and the principles will help you remain focused on your goal of winning business.

Our 24/7 culture forces readers to ask, "what are the most important things to remember in this book?" Authors and consultants always find it hard to simplify what they spend pages writing about. That said, since you can't wait for the arrival of the digital snacks referred to in my acknowledgements, here are what I consider to be the three most important reminders I can give you.

The first is referred to as relationship selling principle #1. We don't have clients, we have relationships. At the end of the day it is people who buy people, not companies that buy companies. I know in B2B we have corporate accounts but when things go wrong it is always because people aren't delivering. Likewise, when you win business it is normally because the sellers won the hearts of the buyers through effective relationship building and communication of value propositions. Some say artificial intelligence will replace all our hard skills, leaving only our soft skills to differentiate us. If that is true, then being good at relationship selling principles is a huge differentiator for success.

The second key concept has to be that the solution is in the dialogue. If you are constantly engaged in dialogue, you will learn what people need and want, how to innovate and provide solutions, how much they are willing to pay for it, and how you can successfully sell your solutions. If you aren't following our dialogue selling process, you should begin. Ensure you engage in five dialogues per day, 25 per week, 100 per month, 1,200 per year. Once you are in dialogue the rest will become easier, but if you are not in dialogue with a lot of people all of the time, you can't possibly do well in business development.

Finally, as you probably recognise by now, having read all the anecdotes shared herein, if you aren't creating a buzz and persisting repeatedly to serve your clients and win business from them, you aren't going to be as successful as those who are. In business development it is the people who spin the fastest and work the hardest that will inevitably produce the most, provided of course they are doing the right thing and have competitive product, service, and value proposition. Don't wait for the world to call you. In the social media today, they suggest three to six posts per day. I recommend five contacts per day, but the important thing is not so much the number as the momentum and consistency. Clients will eventually respond if you are constantly knocking on their doors with the things they need, but if you don't disturb them, you can't blame them for forgetting you. They are just as busy if not more so than you.

I wish you the best of luck with your business development. If you or your team need training, let us know. If you want to teach them the details, buy them all a copy of this book. If you want to crack the whip at your next sales meeting, just ask them about my three points above:

- Comment on the quantity and quality of your relationships.
- Comment on the quality of your dialogues with key stakeholders.
- Comment on the volume of activity or turbulence you are creating in the market.

If you aren't doing well on any of the above points, you can consider this as three strikes: you're out. If you are doing well on all three you are probably hitting home runs, but otherwise focus on the process and principles in this book to brush up on what you might be missing. Any questions, let me know. The solution is in the dialogue. *Bonne chance.*

Appendix I: Relationship Selling Principles

1. You don't have clients you have relationships
2. Relationships cool if not maintained
3. Never cease to develop relationships
4. Some clients can't say yes but don't want to say no
5. Help buyer say no if you realize they won't say yes
6. Make 5 contacts per day
7. Network internally to facilitate cross selling
8. Interrupt relationship building to do your work
9. Don't focus on yourself, focus on the client
10. Respond to the needs of others regardless of payback
11. Ask lots of questions to surface unstated needs
12. Keep building your SECS appeal
13. Ask for business and ask for referral
14. Give client something to remember you
15. Reward those who refer you (appropriately)
16. Say thank you
17. Continuously improve your service & quality
18. Learn all about your competitors
19. Become knowledgeable of all related prices
20. Persist, persist, persist

Appendix II: Dialogue Puzzle

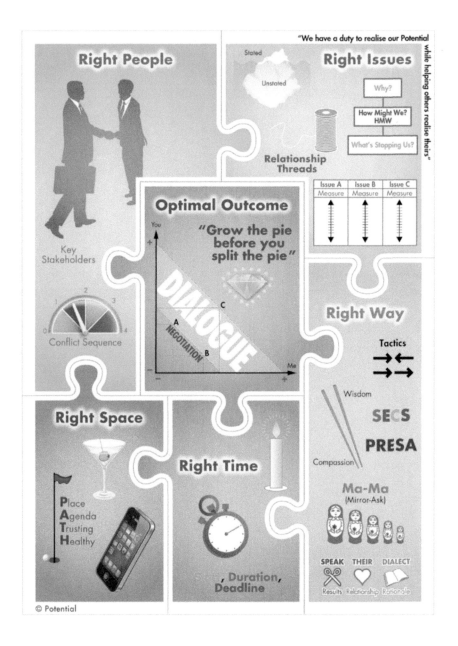

Appendix III: Dialogue Skills – PRESA

The Keys to  Dialogue

1. Control your emotions to enhance your situation rather than hinder it
2. Don't multi-task when in dialogue with others
3. Recognise and listen to your intuition and that of others

4. Be inclusive of others regardless of what diversity separates you
5. Be diplomatic and don't criticise or use judgemental labels
6. Be sincere, honest and dialogue with proper motives

7. Speak your mind and share your feelings without venting rage or anger or lecturing others
8. Inquire appreciatively of others by asking engaging questions without causing bad feelings
9. Don't wait to know it all or get it right before you speak up

10. Be equal in mind and not under obligation to others (egalitarian)
11. Avoid either/or choices & looking at the world as black & white
12. Find compassion for others and accept everything is interdependant

13. Watch people's body language to check if it validates what they are saying
14. Mirror what others say & ask a related question to deepen your understanding (MA-MA 5X)
15. Recognise feedback as a gift regardless of how nicely it is wrapped

Appendix IV: Dialogue Opportunities and Methods

66 Create Opportunities for Dialogue 99

1. Employees focus groups 2. Skip level meetings 3. Lunch with the boss 4. Career development path sharing days 5. Brown bag lunch talks 6. Customer appreciation days 7. Annual strategy sessions and updates 8. Leadership development workshops 9. Award presentations and celebrations 10. One to One with direct reports

66 Choose the Right Dialogue Methodology 99

1. Appreciative Inquiry 2. Brainstorming 3. Challenge Mapping 4. Conversare 5. Drawing Pictures 6. Gestalt 7. Open Space 8. Scenario Planning 9. World Café 10. Mediated Advocacy 11. Dialogue Puzzle

Appendix V: Negotiation Tactics

Push for Results

Double your aspiration point

Persist 3X (at least) with reasons

Set deadlines for others

Reinforce team-mates argument

Re-open previously settled issues

Remind other side you have a choice

Devalue other sides offer (nicely)

Use good guy/bad girl or white/black face

Build Relationships

Talk about common ground

Show compassion to other side

Link your position to people they respect

Use words to express emotions

Offer flexibility then ask how

Offer and invoke reciprocity

Build on common values

Avoid confrontational language

Focus on Details

Ask lots of questions (Ma-Ma 5X)

Recap your understanding

Create issues for give & take

Always link price with package

Offer concessions in small steps (%)

Question assumptions

Link your position with authority

Ask them to justify their position

Use Best Practices

Give examples of value gained

Anchor your range

Prime other party before negotiating

Take a time out whenever needed

Allocate roles/subjects to team-mates

Select venue/set-up purposefully

Agree motivating goal for all

Insist on compliance mechanism

Appendix VI: Conflict De-Escalation Tactics

De-escalate YOUR stress

Behave Differently

1. Do nothing & allow time to better define your reaction
2. Honestly recognise & manage your emotions
3. Meditate: Breath in reflecting on suffering & breath out reflecting on compassion
4. Prepare your concessions: "If I do this...then will you do that?"
5. Remember we are all one
6. Take a time out to calm down
7. Accept accusations & write them down without reacting

Think Differently

8. Practice non-attachment
9. Recognise the impermanence of both the problem and the solution
10. Recognise others suffer and hurt like you
11. Address their motivational style
12. Be polite, your rudeness and anger returns to you intensified
13. Stop seeing the situation as black or white, right or wrong, look for a middle way
14. Ask "Whose needs are being addressed"
15. Stop thinking me vs. you and think us

Open Dialogue

16. Stop, wait, shut-up and listen
17. Ask other party what you don't know
18. Replace your assumptions, accusations and assertions about others with questions to test the correctness of your views
19. Stop your revenge and ask "how can I help this person overcome their strong emotions?"
20. Apologise & admit mistakes

De-escalate THEIR stress

Behave Differently

21. Show patience to others
22. Demonstrate love for others
23. Be compassionate about their situation
24. Smile at anger and don't let it affect you
25. Work together to define the problem
26. Propose solutions hypothetically ("What if we....?")
27. Encourage polite behaviour and reward it when shown by others
28. Replace your anger with diplomacy

Think Differently

29. Share your thinking about the situation
30. Share why you think the way you do

Open Dialogue

31. Encourage them to talk
32. Don't react, explain you are listening and considering next steps
33. Validate their feelings (e.g. "It's ok that you feel this way about me/the situation")
34. Brainstorm alternative solutions
35. Forgive others genuinely
36. Encourage dialogue amongst stakeholders to explore different perspectives before deciding how best to proceed
37. Ask others about themselves, their thoughts and feelings
38. Spend informal time together
39. Ask others if they are intentionally accusing you and if so to provide examples
40. Use a mediator or facilitator to assist difficult dialogues & those involving a lot of stakeholders

Appendix VII: Business Development Roadmap

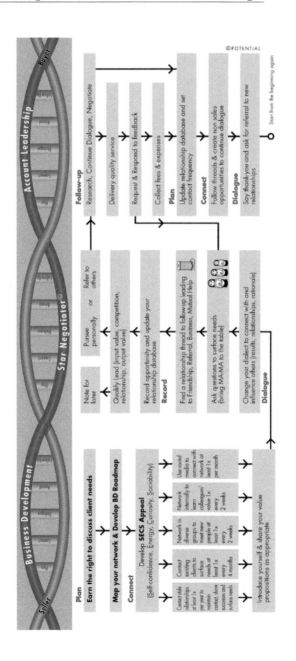

Appendix VIII: Bulldog Opportunity Tracker

Potential **Bulldog Opportunity Tracker** Sheet #_____

Date	
Target Organisation	
Target Person	
Opportunity	
Referrer	
Source	

Appendix IX: RGB Dialect

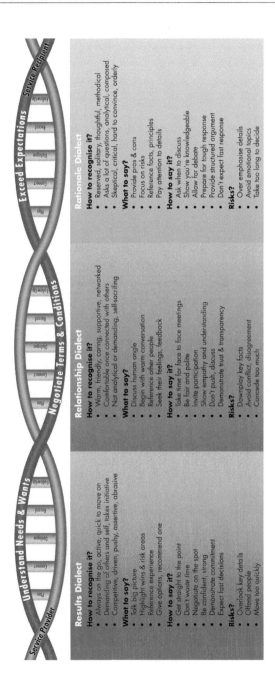

Understand Needs & Wants — Service Provider
Negotiate Terms & Conditions
Exceed Expectations — Service Recipient

(Connect, Plan, Dialogue, Record, Follow-up)

Results Dialect

How to recognise it?
- Always on the go, active, quick to move on
- Demanding of others and self, takes initiative
- Competitive, driven, pushy, assertive, abrasive

What to say?
- Talk big picture
- Highlight wins & risk areas
- Reference experience
- Give options, recommend one

How to say it?
- Get straight to the point
- Don't waste time
- Negotiate on the spot
- Be confident, strong
- Demonstrate commitment
- Expect fast decisions

Risks?
- Overlook key details
- Offend people
- Move too quickly

Relationship Dialect

How to recognise it?
- Warm, friendly, caring, supportive, networked
- Comfortable once connected with others
- Not analytical or demanding, self-sacrifing

What to say?
- Discuss human angle
- Begin with warm conversation
- Reference other people
- Seek their feelings, feedback

How to say it?
- Take time for face to face meetings
- Be fair and polite
- Invite participation
- Show empathy and understanding
- Don't push, discuss
- Demonstrate trust & transparency

Risks?
- Downplay key facts
- Avoid conflict, disagreement
- Concede too much

Rationale Dialect

How to recognise it?
- Reserved, solitary, thoughtful, methodical
- Asks a lot of questions, analytical, composed
- Skeptical, critical, hard to convince, orderly

What to say?
- Provide pros & cons
- Focus on risks
- Reference facts, principles
- Pay attention to details

How to say it?
- Ask when to discuss
- Show you're knowledgeable
- Allow for debate
- Prepare for tough response
- Provide structured argument
- Don't expect fast response

Risks?
- Over emphasise details
- Avoid emotional topics
- Take too long to decide

Appendix X: Top 20 Negotiation Mistakes

1. Accept 1st offer presented
2. Don't prepare people, process & content
3. Accept failure over making concession
4. Don't insist on exchanging concessions
5. Fail to explore improving agreement
6. Insufficient exploration of issues/range
7. Ineffective dialogue & communication
8. Don't take charge of meeting process
9. Lack worthwhile choices/options
10. Mismatch contract, relationships, agreement
11. Overlook key stakeholders/needs
12. Split the difference
13. Mishandle emotions & conflicts
14. Lack authority to negotiate
15. Loose control at documentation stage
16. Fail to make a change when losing control
17. Mismanage time needed & deadlines
18. Don't celebrate achievements together
19. Fail to create trust or relationship
20. Lack tactics in face of opposition

Index

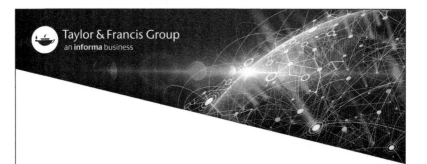